Unsung Heroines

A Practical and Inspirational Book for Pastors' and Leaders' Wives.

General Editor

Alison Chant

Unsung Heroines

A Practical and Inspirational Book for Pastors'
and Leaders' Wives.

Third Edition

ISBN 978-1-61529-223-3

Copyright © 2019 By Vision Christian College

All Rights Reserved Worldwide

Published by Vision Publishing
PO Box 1680
Ramona, CA 92065
760 789-4700
www.booksbyvision.org

Unsung, the noblest deed will die."

Pindar (c. 518- c. 438 BC) Fragment 120

Pindar was the chief lyric poet of Greece. In his poem he gives advice and reproof as well as praise to his patrons. This line from one of his works shows an insight into our human condition. We all need to be affirmed by someone. No matter how strong we are in character, each one of us needs to know that our efforts are known and appreciated.

I would like to dedicate this book to all the unsung heroines of modern times and pray that when that great day comes and we receive the tender word of Jesus, *"Well done, good and faithful servant"*, we will be content.

Foreword

As I have read through this amazing book, I have found myself relating to some of the different areas that I have been through over more than 40 years of ministry as a Pastor's Wife.

I would recommend this book to anyone who is a Pastor's Wife, past, present or just starting out.

Being a Pastor's Wife is not just supporting your husband but is a ministry to the Lord in its own right. We are particular vessels for the Lord, but are often loaded with all sorts of unwanted cargo, leaving us wondering how to stay afloat. However, on the other hand, there are also the many blessings that override the negatives.

What Alison has drawn from the lives, challenges and victories of the many Pastors' Wives over the years, gives insight and encouragement to those who are facing similar situations. Through this book they will find a greater confidence in the Lord to move forward.

Thank you, Alison!

Joy Whatnall

Preface to the Third Edition

In this preface to the third edition I would like to point out that twenty years have passed since the first edition was published. Many changes have been made in the church since then and many more women are taking on the task of working as pastor for a congregation.

Some scholars agree this is a good thing, but others are wary that the church will be changed to a significant extent should this trend continue to expand until there are more women than men in the ministry.

Meantime, in Australia other changes have made it easier for pastors' wives to be trained and supported by their contemporaries. Pastors' wives are encouraged to study and there are now special times for pastors' wives to get together and share and support one another.

One other significant change has been made. A pastor's wife is now encouraged to become a pastor in her own right, ordained and working alongside her husband in the ministry.

Since this book was first printed there have been some radical changes in church life, and there will be many more in the future as the church struggles to maintain its place in a world that is changing so dramatically.

I would like to thank all those who contributed to this book now in its third edition. Special thanks to Joan Beard, Heather Eaton, Sharon Jones, Lois Cronin, Liz Bailey, Gwen Leane, Vanessa Chant, Moya Enright and our missionary contributor Jana Locke.

May the Lord bless all those in church leadership today who seek to serve God faithfully.

Alison Chant

Table of Contents

The Foundation for Unsung Heroines

Twenty years ago, I decided to write a helpful book for other pastors' wives like myself who were struggling to understand what their role should be. By then I had been a pastor's wife for many years and learned many things.

I will never forget the very first Ladies Meeting I had to conduct. I was twenty years of age and had taken no notice of such meetings up until that time. I had been interested in Youth Meetings. Ladies Meetings were for older women.

Why hadn't someone prepared me for this!

My husband Ken, then an eager young pastor, had boundless faith in my abilities.

"You'll be fine dear", he said, *"no problem!"*

The fact that I was very pregnant at the time didn't help matters but somehow, I muddled through, feeling totally inadequate.

No one had ever given me any advice. It wasn't until four years later I was to receive any advice on being a pastor's wife, and then it was merely a heart stopping declaration -

"You realise that you can either make or break your husband's ministry."

That was it!

Over the years I learned many things; how to conduct a meeting, give a Bible Study, lead in worship, but what a pity I could not have been taught all the things I needed to know earlier. I could have been far more effective and could have been saved many a stumble!

I would have had a far better self-image, had more confidence, suffered less heartache, helped more people, and been of more use to the family of God.

These days pastors' wives are far better prepared. Or are they? I decided to find out for myself and prepared a questionnaire, which I have been handing out to my peers over these last two years.

Some of the information I have compiled and some of the helpful hints I have in this book I owe to these very wonderful and godly ladies. Some of them have contributed a chapter or a testimony, others have provided notes, and many have helped with research.

When you are a pastor's wife you learn to laugh a lot otherwise you might cry too much. It can be a wonderful life if you don't mind watching your husband being moulded by the hand of God and circumstances, and by God's wonderful, beautiful, sometimes mixed up, courageous, impossible saints.

Perhaps there should be classes for future pastors' wives and for other church leaders' wives. Classes to teach them public speaking, people skills, singing, Bible study preparation, dress sense, hospitality, economy, children's ministry, according to their interests. Think of the confidence they would gain. It would enhance their husband's ministry and perhaps double and triple his usefulness to the kingdom of God.

What would I have liked to know when I first began? What would I like to tell others who are just beginning? These are the things I have tried to present to you in this book.

Alison Chant

Chapter One

A Unique Life!

One day, through a misunderstanding, my husband and I arrived at a pastor's home for dinner. Five minutes later the family arrived home from a two-week holiday at the beach! They would not hear of us leaving, nor would they allow us to order a Pizza or any other fast food item. I must admit I was most impressed by that pastor and his wife.

In hospitality he was everything a pastor should be, she was everything a pastor's wife should be. She not only made us welcome, she cooked a lovely meal while organizing her household, answering the telephone, and attending to her children.

He unpacked their car, made us coffee, set the table, and entertained us with lively conversation. It was all done seemingly effortlessly. Their names? Richard and Chris Murray of Canberra.

We have been entertained in many homes because of our travelling ministry, and pastors and pastors' wives are always gracious, kind and hospitable. Hospitality is a part of the gifting of God for a pastor and his wife.

But it is not the only part of the unique life of working as a pastor and attending to the flock of God. In recent months psychiatrists and counsellors have been examining the life of the pastor's wife and they have come to some startling conclusions.

Here is one of them!

As those in the ministry know, Protestant pastors' wives are unique in the extent to which they are impacted by their spouse's vocation. Clergy marriages are highly visible, closely scrutinized by community members, and frequently looked to as the models for Christian marriage.[1]

Results of Survey

One of the most interesting results of the survey that pastors' wives have completed for me this year has been the number who have discovered, as I did myself in the first few years of ministry, that it is impossible to please everybody in the church. In fact, the more you try the less successful you become! The reason is simple. Everyone wants something different from you and so in trying to please all you finish by annoying everyone.

My conclusion, and that of many others, was to be true to yourself and God's will for your life and leave everyone else to accommodate themselves to that as they are able. In fact, the single most frequent answer to the question, *"What helpful advice would you give to a new pastor's wife?"* was *"Be yourself!"*

The truth is pastors' wives are just the same as all other Christian women, with some strength and some weakness, and the same needs, emotions, trials and responsibilities. Their difference lies in two directions: one is that their congregation expects so much from them; and the other is that their marriage and family are so highly visible.

Invent as You Go?

This week I read something in our daily paper which caught my attention. It was a description of the life of an Australian Prime Minister's wife. The similarity to the life of a pastor's wife was irresistible. Here is the quote:

It's a job you invent as you go, and all hell breaks

---

[1] Alleman D. Art. *WMM's A New Kind of Model*, Theology News and Notes. December 1990

loose if you make a mistake. There's no training course, no job description, no pay and relentless public scrutiny. Nobody is ever satisfied: feminists want you to speak out, and traditionalists expect you to act like a 'lady'. [2]

When you have had no training, you must invent as you go, and in this modern age the rules are changing. Some pastors are expecting their wife to partner them in their ministry far more than when I first began my life as a pastor's wife, but until recently there has been no-one to teach or train young women who have been faced with the daunting task of beginning a ministry with their husbands; at least not in most Non-Denominational, Pentecostal or Independent churches.

Other pastors' wives are being left free to pursue their own careers outside of the church altogether. However, tradition has called for the pastor's wife to become involved in church work to support her spouse, or because she felt she should.

Changes are in the air in the USA among the mainline churches. I'm not sure that I agree with them, but these are the kinds of things that are happening.

Some of the wives are attending other churches and even other denominations; others have no religious affiliation at all. Some of them have a career which takes them to other places for days or even weeks at a time. Some of them are pastors themselves in another church. Others have become hospital chaplains.

Regardless of the amount of involvement or non-involvement pastors' wives who are happiest are those who have a good self image and are pleased with their own life and career options.

---

[2] Landmore D. *Prime Ministers' Wives*; McPhee Gribble, 1992.

A congregation may expect each new pastor's wife to conform to the previous pastor's wife, even though she may be a
totally different personality with her own unique gifts. It is
unfair to expect conformity, or uniformity, in each case.

An Idealised View

The people usually have an idealized view of what a pastor's
family life should be like. If they try to force those beliefs on
the pastor and his family all kinds of stresses and strains may
develop. Especially if a pastor's family do try to conform to
the unreal expectations of their own congregation.

In our own country of Australia we have a multi-cultural
society, each culture with its own idea of what a pastor and
his family should be doing, and how they should live and
conduct themselves, as Susan discovered.

"What are we going to do?" she cried to her husband,
*"Everyone will find out about the divorce our daughter is
going through. What will they think? Will we lose our
ministry? Will the people understand? I just can't bear
anyone to know about it!"* Her husband sighed heavily.
Compassion for his wife and daughter mixed with
apprehension for the future. What would his church people
say? Would they ask him to move on? He drew his wife to
him and gave her an understanding hug. *"Perhaps we can
put in for a transfer, and then we will not have to tell
anyone about it."*

Susan was facing the dilemma of her daughter's divorce,
wondering how it would affect her husband's ministry, or
whether the church would insist that he leave the ministry
because he could not manage his family. Also, she felt all the
shame of people gossiping about their daughter's failed
marriage.

Three Major Difficulties

Perfection

There are three major difficulties facing the pastor's wife: the first involves the pressure to be perfect, a perfect wife, a perfect mother, and a perfect pastor's wife!

This can be very wearing. The stress of keeping up appearances, of always striving to live up to all expectations, of hiding any traumas and hurts within the family, can be exhausting. At least three quarters of pastors' wives feel this pressure, to be ideal role models of motherhood and Christian family life.

If you accept these pressures and try to live them out you will be filled with resentment, feel a failure, and finally burn out. What is more important, your children will suffer and may never recover. Christianity will become to them a thing of hypocrisy, an impossible dream, not connected to reality.

You must learn to please God, to please your husband and your children, and to let the people find their level of acceptance of you and your family.

Don't let others set your agenda for you. Be an actor not a reactor, being pulled here and there by others. Decide who you are, what your gifts are, and then ask God to guide you into what he wants you to do.

Remember the words of Jesus,

> *I tell you the truth, the Son can do nothing by himself; he can do only what he sees his Father doing, because whatever the Father does the Son also does (Jn 5:19).*

Say to yourself, *"What does God want of me,"* and then live accordingly. In this way you will be living honestly, not in deception, and because of this you will be able to deal quickly with any hurts or problems, which arise from time to time in any family.

Managing Children

Mary groaned and heaved a big sigh; the children were fighting again. She could hear them out on the patio. They seemed to fight 'non-stop,' she hadn't had a minute to herself for days. Having the children quickly had been her idea, now she had three under five and she wasn't so sure it had been a good decision after all. She had come from a family where the children were born many years apart and she had always regretted not being close to her siblings.

Sometimes, on days like this one, she really resented her husband being a pastor.

"I should have married a farmer or perhaps a plumber", she mused, *"And then perhaps I'd get some help with the children, especially in the evenings."*

When Peter came home, excited about what God was doing in his ministry, she would try not to cry. It wasn't fair; she would like to be out there too, ministering to people; that was one of the reasons she had been so thrilled when Peter had asked her to marry him.

Peter tried to understand, but he too was beginning to resent her attitude.

"Why can't she be happy with what God is doing", he thought to himself. *"She used to be such a happy person and on fire for God."*

Sometimes, like Mary, we can feel left out of ministry. Especially when we have little ones, and consider we aren't helping our husbands or doing anything significant for God.

Keeping your home is your ministry; while they are young your children are your ministry.

A significant verse was given to me by the Lord many years ago, and afterwards it was confirmed to me by Rev. Dick

Mills.

> *The share of the man who stayed with the supplies is to be the same as that of him who went down to the battle. All shall share alike (1Sa 30:24).*

This was a decision made by David when some of his men, who had suffered the heat of a battle, wanted to keep all the spoil instead of sharing it with those whom David had asked to stay by their equipment and protect it.

What does this mean for us? Simply this; those of us who cannot, (for whatever reason), share in our husband's public ministry will share in his reward on that great day when we stand before the judgment seat of Christ.

Friendships

The second problem we face is what to do about friendships. Many pastors' wives have no close friendships within their church. They feel awkward about making close friends from among the congregation in case it leads to jealousy.

This idea of having no close friends within the church leads inevitably to isolation. It is difficult to have intimate friend-ships. A guard must be kept on your lips, you must be careful not to betray confidences.

In my own life I have tended to be quiet, not very talkative, mainly because I have learned it is safer that way. I learned discretion in the school of hard knocks! In early days I made mistakes by speaking when it would have been better to have remained silent. So, in reaction, I became very careful of my speech. *"Least said, soonest mended."* This is an old and wise saying, which I have tried to make a habit.

Even so I have made many close friendships over the years with other women in the church. They shared my joys and sorrows during the years I was growing and maturing, having my children, and learning to love and serve God. We shared picnics and parties, had our babies at around the same time, and shared our baby clothes as we shared our trials. We learned together what it means to be a godly wife and mother.

My husband worked in the same church for 16 of his 26 years as a local pastor, and that enabled us to make deep friendships. It would be difficult to make similar friendships now that we are moving constantly in a teaching ministry.

If I am asked, *"Who is my best friend?"* I would have to say, *"It is my husband!"* We have never felt the need for other intimate friendships as some people do, though this has not stopped us from building many delightful and loving friendships with godly people.

One caution needs to be aired. Always be prudent and careful not to share intimate details of your life with anyone. There are some things which should remain with your spouse and no one else. Be careful too, not to expose your children's lives to others; be sensitive to their feelings.

Be careful of your reason for choosing a friendship. Are you using a friend to denigrate your husband or to criticize others in the church? This can be devastating. Sometimes we need to air our hurts and deal with problems, but if this is so then it should be as a means of showing forgiveness and to restore relationships, not just to air our grievances.

To come together with a group of women for mutual support and encouragement is a healthy and wise thing to do. During our years in San Diego, USA, Pastor Pamela Truscott began a pastors' wives support group, which we held once a month. It was touching to see the younger pastors' wives come to that meeting, seemingly happy and tranquil, but before long one or other of them would be pouring out her heart and revealing deep hurts, which needed our prayers and our compassion and some wise words from those older and more experienced.

Being a pastor's wife is not easy, and if we are not careful to choose some good friends in whom we can trust we can become deeply hurting individuals in desperate need of support and encouragement. Praise God he is always there for us; but we also need some kind friends who understand; peers who can teach us the things we need to know.

Indeed, each pastor's family needs some friends from outside their church with whom they can relax. Because of the busy life they lead too many pastors and their families become isolated from any friendships with people from their community. Neighbours in turn can be puzzled by this and feel the pastor's family are proud and unfriendly.

Intrusion

Our third problem is that our husband's ministry seems to intrude into every part of our lives. The ministry seems never ending, it goes on constantly, day and night, day after day, every day.

For many years my husband and I lived without a structured ministry life. The ministry ran us; we allowed other people to dictate the time and place of ministry. After years of this total dedication we realised we needed to preserve our health and our family life; and we began to educate the people. It took some time but once it was established that appointments needed to be made for counseling, people soon became used to the new way of doing things and stopped complaining.

Sometimes of course there is an emergency and we must go; but normally people's problems take time to develop, and it will not hurt if they cannot see a counselor for a day or so.

I learned some truthful, though neutral words for the telephone.

"I'm sorry, but the pastor is not available just now. May I take a message?"

It is no concern of anyone just exactly what your husband happens to be doing at that moment. He could be having his dinner, playing with his children, counseling someone else; no matter, he is simply *"not available."*

How I wish that someone had taught me those simple words. It would have saved much time, and how much more rested and relaxed my family would have been. People do not mean to intrude; they may 'phone at the dinner hour because they realise you will be at home then. Unfortunately, what they do not realise is that they are one of many who are trying to contact the pastor. Too many evenings our meals were interrupted and grew cold because of ministry. Nowadays with mobile phones we have more control of our time.

We must learn that most ministry can wait. People's problems can usually wait 24 hours without too much trauma. They have probably been a long time forming and a few more hours won't make much difference to the outcome unless it is a genuine emergency.

Pastors are realising more and more that they need to spend quality time with their wives and children. If they do, then family life will be happy and secure; if they don't, they will reap a bitter harvest.

Many pastors' wives feel emotionally deprived because of their husband's total involvement in ministry. They don't complain, because how can they admit they are 'jealous of God'. The children also become hurt and bewildered when their father keeps putting meetings and other people before their legitimate needs. Their self image suffers; and because their father is, in a sense, their role model of what God is like, they grow up with the impression that God is too busy for them, a remote figure, someone who doesn't really care how they feel.

A Messiah Complex

Why do pastors get so absorbed in ministry? One reason is a messiah complex. This is the idea that they, and they alone, are capable of doing the work, rescuing the people; bringing them deliverance, and so on.

Then there is sometimes a need for him to escape from problems in his home and family, especially if his wife is attempting to make him see he is neglecting them. If he doesn't want to face the discussions, he will make sure he is always too busy to talk. He may find he is unable to say, "*No*", to people; or he may feel he has to do everything, because no one else can do it well enough.

We went through many of these stages and we could have been saved from many errors, if only someone had told us in the beginning of our ministry the things to watch for and avoid.

Neglected

In his article Duane Alleman lists five things a wife of a busy pastor can do to overcome the feelings of neglect she has because her husband is over-involved in ministry.[3]

The list is his, the comments are mine.

1. Identify her feelings: How is her husband's busy ministry affecting her, and their children, and their family life together?

2. Clarify her expectations and desires: What does she want, what is a reasonable life style, what can she expect? She must be specific so that a compromise can be worked out.

3. Communicate her feelings and desires directly: I remember a mistake I frequently made when we were first married. I would brood over some task not done, some neglect, and then when I had bottled it up for several weeks I would burst out with, "*I wish you would do so and so...!*"

---

3 Alleman D. art. *WMM's A New Kind Of Model;* Theology News and Notes, Dec 1990.

My poor husband, in all ignorance that I had been feeling these things, would be overwhelmed by my outburst. After this had happened a few times he lovingly asked me to please tell him in a reasonable manner when he had made an error. Instead of, "I wish..." would I say, "Darling would you do so and so...?"

We got along much better after I learned this appropriate response!

4. Seek out other relationships: Do not expect your husband to meet all your needs. He is not God. It is draining for him if you are continually expecting him to be the sole input into your life. The Lord knows your needs, and if you pray, he will guide you into friendships that will add to you and cause you to be a strength to your husband. This will help to build him up also.

5. Seek help: If after taking all these precautions you still feel all is not well, then you need to get some help. Don't be afraid to seek out a Christian counselor, someone you can trust, someone who is not too close to either of you so that he/she can see things more clearly. It may save your marriage and your husband's ministry.

Helpful Books

Dale Garrett, *The Pleasure of Your Company;* Kingsway Publications.

Florence Littauer, *Personality Plus;* Fleming H. Revell 1983.

Don and Katie Fortune, *Discover Your God Given Gifts.*

Cameron Lee, *Life in a Glasshouse;*

Bart & Tony Campolo, *Things We Wish We Had Said;* Word Books.

Hannah Whitall Smith, *The Christian's Secret of a Happy Life;* Fleming H. Revell.

Cecil Osborne, *The Art of Understanding Yourself;* plus *The Art of Understanding Your Mate;* Zondervan.

David Fontana, *Know Who You Are, Be What You Want;* Fontana, Harpers Collins Publishers, 1992.

Chapter Two

Helpful Teaching

Before I begin to write this chapter, I would like to point out that these are some of the things I would like to have known before I became a pastor's wife. You may have a different list and may have other ideas of the necessities I feel led to mention here. I am now 70 years of age so some of my ideas may seem archaic to those of you that are younger and have grown up in a different world. If so, I would like to hear from you.

Your Own Development

Love the Lord your God with all your heart and with all your soul and with all your mind. This is the first and greatest commandment. And the second is like it: Love your neighbour as yourself. All the law and the prophets hang on these two commandments (Ma 22:37-38).

Loving God like this is the first and foremost desire of every Christian and the ultimate ideal. However, true perfection awaits the resurrection and meanwhile we will be wise if we are content to be clay in the hands of our heavenly Potter (Is 45:9).

So be yourself! Have confidence in your own abilities. Don't try to please everyone. Cultivate a good self-image. Learn who you are, your temperament and motivational gifts; learn to flow in those things that are right and easy for you.

I remember how freeing it was for me to discover that I was a mercy person with a servant heart. It explained why I was no good as a leader. I used to wonder why I could not easily organise people to do things. I was always far happier doing everything for myself, and never happier than when I was serving others. Also, I was not much good at uncovering or dealing with sin in people's lives, I had far rather not know about their sins which is characteristic of a person with a mercy motive.

Over the years I have studied and gained my master's degree in Christian counseling and have become more of a teacher. I still love to serve my husband and family, but no longer feel the compulsion to serve anyone and everyone as I used to do. I have discovered the truth that we can develop and change as we mature.

If there are jobs to be done and you don't feel able, then perhaps you can delegate, or pray someone else in to do the task that needs doing. Try not to be bound by the expectations of others, either for yourself, your husband, or your children. Instead work on pleasing God and your husband, satisfying your children, and allowing yourself to grow and mature slowly but surely into other tasks you feel capable of doing.

Keep a good sense of humour, learn to laugh at yourself. Don't take life so seriously that you have a breakdown. Have lots of fun, balance your life, do something every week that has nothing to do with people or problems! Take up a hobby, play a sport, or improve your education.

On Starting as the New Pastor in an Established Church

These are some of the things we learnt over the twenty-five years we were in pastoral ministry.

It was he (Jesus) who gave some to be apostles, some to be prophets, some to be evangelists, and some to be pastors and teachers, to prepare God's people for works of service, so that the body of Christ may be built up until we all reach unity in the faith and in the knowledge of the Son of God and

become mature, attaining to the whole measure of
the fullness of Christ (Ep 4:11-13).

These ministry gifts are given to the church, but they need to be recognised by those in charge of the church. There are three periods of ministry a pastor goes through while he is settling in and getting to know his people.

The Honeymoon Period

In the first few months the new pastor appears perfect to the congregation and he can do no wrong! This is a good time to make changes, though not too many and not too quickly. Everyone is attempting to gain the new pastor's favour, a very happy time!

The Settling Down Period

The pastor begins to know his people and the people begin to know their pastor and to see he is not as perfect as they thought at first. This can still be a good time but 'give and take' are essential. Adjustments need to be made on both sides. If the pastor is secure within himself then he can accept and deal with criticism, changing where necessary and scriptural. The people's criticisms need to be taken into consideration as much as possible within the framework of 'true Christianity', otherwise they will lose heart and 'vote with their feet', that is, leave the church and go to another one. However, the congregation should not expect their new pastor to be a carbon copy of the last one. He is his own man with his own gifts and abilities in God. Time must be given to get to know and appreciate the new ministry. How much time? This varies but can take up to two or even three years.

The Mature Relationship Period

This is the time when everyone has settled down into their role and the church can begin moving and doing something for God. The pastor has assessed his people and knows their capabilities and ministries and where he can fit them into the church life. Communication should then be free and full flowing as the people share in the ongoing ministry of the church. Together the congregation and the pastor can do great things for God.

On Starting a New Church

It is not good for a couple to go out alone to build a new church. They need at least one other couple to share the work, the prayer, the expenses and the set-backs, as well as the triumphs.

A new church may be a house church. If the services are held in the pastor's home, then this can cause a great lack of privacy; even more so if the home is owned by the church. People may feel they can visit at any time of the day or evening.

Lack of money can cause friction. In Non-Denominational and Pentecostal churches pastors must be content with less money than other men who have studied the same length of time. They must build a new church until it is large enough to support them with a decent wage. In the mean-time, the wife may become bitter and resentful. She can go out to work, but if she does have a career this can be held up because she cannot move when necessary. It takes a woman called of God to help build a new church!

Courtesy

Therefore, as God's chosen people, holy and dearly loved, clothe yourselves with compassion, kindness, humility, gentleness, and patience. Bear with each other and forgive whatever grievances you may have against one another. Forgive as the Lord forgave you. And over all these virtues put on love, which binds them all together in perfect unity. Let the peace of Christ rule in your hearts, since as members of one body you were called to peace (Cl 3:12-15).

This scripture refers to the church, the body of Christ, but in a sense the family is also a 'little church' therefore this scripture refers also to the family. It is love which binds every member together in perfect harmony both in the individual families of the church and in the whole church family.

> Some people think that the closer they are to another person the less courtesy they need to show. The reverse is true. The closer you are to others the more essential good manners are to the ongoing relationship. [4]

Good manners should be practised daily in the home. If your children hear you being polite, they will automatically copy you in time.

When I was doing my nursing training, I was taught not to raise my voice unless there was a fire or other accident! I feel this is a good idea as a calm home can be so restful. Of course, there can be riotous times of fun and frolic within the family in a happy, joyful sense. We all need these moments of happiness, but voices raised in anger can be so wounding to all concerned.

Talk politely to one another, compliment frequently and sincerely. Be considerate of each other's feelings; learn tact and diplomacy unless these come naturally to you. Think before you speak. Is this necessary, is it kind?

> Sometimes fathers and mothers treat their grown-up children with an incivility, which, offered to any other young people would simply have terminated the acquaintance. [5]

As our children grow and mature into their teenage years, we

---

[4] Oliver Wendell Holmes.

[5] C. S. Lewis, *"The Four Loves"*

need to continue to treat them with courtesy if we want them to honour us and retain close family ties.

Church Manners

> *To the elders among you, I appeal as a fellow elder, a witness of Christ's sufferings and one who also will share in the glory to be revealed. Be shepherds of God's flock that is under your care, serving as overseers - not because you must, but because you are willing, as God wants you to be; not greedy for money, but eager to serve; not lording it over those entrusted to you, but being examples to the flock. And when the Chief Shepherd appears, you will receive the crown of glory that will never fade away. Young men, in the same way be submissive to those who are older. Clothe yourselves with humility towards one another, because, 'God opposes the proud but gives grace to the humble' (1Pe 5:1-5).*

Some people are just naturally likeable and affable toward others. The rest of us need to be taught people skills!

I remember several things I used to do which hurt peoples' feelings. I would walk up to a group of people and begin to speak to one person and ignore the others. When I was busy doing something, I would look up as someone entered the room then go on with my work without greeting them. Finally, someone pointed these things out to me, and this was a great help. It does not take a moment to greet a group of people before you begin to speak to one of them. It only takes a second to greet someone who has walked into a room before you continue with your work, but these little courtesies make all the difference to the self esteem of members of your congregation.

Smile often, be aware!

Use courtesy toward your husband; don't discuss him with

the members of your church. If the need arises, always lift him up in the estimation of the people; never criticise him in public. If you are desperate for advice, talk to one of his peers, one you can trust, preferably someone far enough distant not to be emotionally involved with the problem, one who can speak with wisdom, but not someone who could profit from exposing your husband's faults.

We also need wisdom in the way we conduct ourselves toward visitors to the church and to those people we meet from day to day, so that we may attract them to Christ, as Paul directs in Colossians.

> *Be wise in the way you act towards outsiders; make the most of every opportunity. Let your conversation be always full of grace, seasoned with salt, so that you may know how to answer everyone (Cl 4:5).*

If you are working in a small church, then greet new people and introduce them to at least one other person. If you are in a larger church, then you may have ushers and deacons to take on this task for you.

Be tactful and courteous to all, though it is only natural that you will feel closer to those of your own age and cultural background. Even so it may be better not to have any close favourites within the church body. This is something you will have to work out for yourself.

How to Cope When People Leave Your Church

Depending on the reason why people leave your church you can have different feelings. If they are moving away because of a new job or for some other legitimate reason, then you will feel loss but no grief or rejection. If they leave because of criticism or because of some problem, then you may feel grief, rejection, bewilderment and sorrow.

How do you cope with these feelings? Listen to the words of

the Psalmist,

> *The righteous cry out, and the Lord hears them; he delivers them from all their troubles. The Lord is close to the broken hearted and saves those who are crushed in spirit. A righteous man may have many troubles, but the Lord delivers him from them all (Ps 34:17-19).*

First you should accept the feelings, accept the fact, talk over your reactions with a trusted friend, and then leave the people concerned with God. Let him work it out. Love the people and let them go with your blessing. Better they go than they stay and cause problems in the church family.

What if they take others with them?

Continue to pray for them all and leave them in God's hands. If they leave, then they have removed themselves from your church family; they are no longer your responsibility. If you release them then God will be able to deal with them, if that is necessary.

For yourself, make sure that you work through any feelings of bitterness and grief. As Jesus tells us in Mark's gospel,

> *And when you stand praying, if you hold anything against anyone, forgive him, so that your Father in heaven may forgive you your sins (Mk 11:25 see also Ma 5:23&24).*

If you are sure there is nothing you can do, or need to do, in the way of reconciliation put the whole experience behind you, then go on to love and assist those people who do love you and fellowship with you. If you should meet the person or persons socially after they have left your church, then treat them with courtesy.

*Since I wrote those words of wisdom, acquired over many years, I have received a booklet on this very theme and have been given permission to add it to this book. It was written by Gwen Leane and Liz Bailey on the request of their denomination and delivered at a Conference in 1994 (Liz Bailey has more to say in *Ministry Pressures in a Nutshell* and *Addendum Two,* later in this book).

The Booklet begins -

Dear Lord, I've Got a Splitting Heartache!

"You have my total support mate," said a member to the pastor. Next day he had left the church without a word to anyone. *"It's the people who speak support and then betray us,"* said Jane. Her reaction was one of pain and anger.

Eventually Jane realised that the important thing was to keep a right relationship with the Lord. *"The Lord is my strength; of whom shall I be afraid?"* was a key verse that strengthened and encouraged her.

There isn't a pastor's wife alive who is not familiar with such a scene as this.

1. Failure – The loss of people from fellowship is like the death of a loved one. A sense of having failed in some way is felt. The defection of members is seen as a personal attack on the pastor and his wife. A sense of rejection arises, and self-esteem is at an all time low.

2. Anger – The feeling that God has forsaken his servant occurs. There is no answer from a brassy heaven. A feeling of helplessness at being unable to solve the problem as a person of God takes over.

3. Hurt – Hurt is experienced for the members who remain faithful and for the members who leave.

4. Betrayal – A sense of being used and duped into thinking all is well when it isn't, doesn't do much towards a loving attitude. Misplaced trust is a heart hardener.

5. Sorrow – The deep sense of loss over a loved one and the grief and shame of having the family split apart senselessly, can be experienced. The loss of close relationships can feel like a cutting knife. One woman said: "*I cried for a month*". Reviewing old photos and church videos can cause the memory of the pain to resurface.

6. Snowballing effect – One family or person leaving can be unsettling to others. Breaking ranks sometimes has a psychological effect, similar to the 'domino effect'. There are always a percentage of people who are disgruntled. They identify and side with those who leave and criticise the church. This further unsettles people.

7. Counselees – Often people you spend the most time helping are the first to leave. Statistics show that those who obtain deep counseling can leave later because they feel exposed. For us, it's painful to feel used. It's painful to feel their ingratitude. It's painful to see them used in other churches after we've brought them through to wholeness!

Fortunately, there are steps that can be taken to help these very human reactions, steps toward peace of mind, a pure heart and an obedient spirit.

1. Perspective – Firstly perspective is essential, seeing the situation from God's point of view. Time is the ingredient needed at this point.

2. Letting go – As members leave the church, we must release them. Not to do so prolongs the agony. Trust them to God. He will take them forward. Releasing people is a way of guarding our own hearts from bitterness (Pr 4:23). Also, the principle of death to self operates in these situations. Out of death comes a closer walk with God. Out of death people skills are learnt. Out of death we grow into the likeness of the Lord Jesus Christ. Out of death comes regrowth in the church.

3. Encouragement – We need friends in the ministry outside our own local church. A pastor and his wife need the support of each other. Only a peer can fully understand the pain, especially of the senior pastor's wife.

4. Forgiveness – This is important (Mt 18:22) Do not take hurt into your spirit. Of course, feelings can't be denied, they need to be expressed rather than repressed. The secret is our knowing the depth of God's forgiveness toward us. We are then better able to extend forgiveness in the face of deep hurt. Another secret is talking to God about it. Use him as your sounding board for your hurt, betrayal and anger. He's been there and done that for you and me. He understands!

5. Anchorage – The pain experienced when people leave the church will serve to anchor us into God. It's easy for us to feel that the defection of members is a personal attack. Reality recognises these experiences are *"that I might know him and the fellowship of his suffering, being made conformable to his death."* (Ph 3:10).

6. Thankfulness – This is essential. We need to understand deep in our spirit that *"all things work together for good, to those who love God and are fitting into his plans* (Ro 8:28).

Hold the members of your church body loosely. We should not be so dependent on people being around forever. The church belongs to God. Our attitudes to negative situations can be altered when we change our viewpoint and see that it was great that they were with us for as long as they were...rather than mourning the fact that they will no longer be with us. When we keep this focus, the door of fellowship is left open and should the defectors wish to return they can.

7. Resettlement – Sometimes it is practical to assist them in settling into their new church. Some pastors write references of their good qualities. Continue to love them – let them know it by your caring attitude.

8. The pastor's children – Guard your children as much as possible from the pain, the rejection and the grief (that you are experiencing). Rob and Liz Bailey have been told by

the pastors' children (at the camps they run) that the
children suffer deeply, seeing their parents suffer. They find
it hard to cope emotionally when their parents confide their
hurts and their conflicts (See *Addendum Two*).

9. Bless them – do all you can to try and heal the situation
before they leave, so they go on a positive note. It's easier
then when you meet them again! But don't try to hold onto
them once they decide to leave – they can become like a
festering sore. If their heart is not with you it's better for all if
they leave.

10. Whose church? – It's not ours! We do not own the
people! Jesus said, *"I will build my church"* (Mt 16:18).
"Unless the Lord build the house" (Ps 27:1).

11. Our minds – We need to take control of our thought life
(2 Co 10:4-5). If we let our mind and imagination run
rampant, it will only bring us further pain. Such as going
over and over past conversations, living in regret and 'if
only's'. Self-pity can rule us if we allow it.

12. It happens in all churches – Recognize that you did
your best. Not everyone can have their needs met in your
church. We are a consumer society. People 'shop around'. It's
part of the Australian culture, some churches become flavour
of the month in their district. People sometimes feel they are
ready to move onto another training ground, to make them
complete. Others leave to escape God's challenge. Remember
we only have them on loan. We can't have a possessive
attitude.

13. Rejection – We need to work on not taking it personally. If the church and being the pastor's wife is where
your self-image is based, look out! When church numbers go
down, they take your self-image down with it. We need to
centre our identity in Jesus. We are still lovable, precious
and accepted because God's Word says so. It helps to have an
identity and interests outside of the church. Such as hobbies,

sports, employment, shopping etc.

14. Evaluate – It's time to reassess. Why did they leave? Did we do anything wrong? Can we improve? We must learn to give objective answers to these questions. It's so easy to blame the leavers, or the devil. We need to make it a learning, growing experience. Feelings of failure are soothed by Jesus' love.

15. Husbands – Our reactions can affect him. Reaction only adds pressure to a husband who is himself struggling in a no-win situation. We need to be a source of encouragement, a shield. Give him time to collect himself. Be a buffer, initially – provide space, and time. We can feed the situation; add fuel to the fire with our emotions and recriminations. Some couples find it best to discuss the situation late at night, in their bedroom. Others find it devastating to dwell on painful, controversial or stressful topics just prior to going to sleep. But it can serve to bind you in a closer relationship with your husband as you go through the pain with him.

16. Summing up – Having followed the principles pray all the time. Ask God for anything in line with the Holy Spirit's wishes. Plead with him, remind him of your needs and keep praying earnestly for all Christians everywhere (Ep 6:18).

End of booklet.

What Kind of Home Should You Have?

> ... *train the younger women to love their husbands and children, to be self controlled and pure, to be busy at home, to be kind, and to be subject to their husbands, so that no one will malign the word of God (Tit 2:4-5).*

Your home needs to be a place of refuge, solace, and peace for your family. Somewhere they can find rest; for refreshment and refueling, both spiritually and materially. It should be moderately clean and well managed as there will be visitors. It is good to have a hospitable home; but you should never feel ashamed or embarrassed if you have no expensive food for casual callers. Bread and butter and a cup of coffee or tea will suffice. If people come unexpectedly then they must accept what you have. If you invite people, then of course more will be expected.

Your home should be well ordered. A hundred years ago, some pastors' wives had at least one house maid, possibly a cook, and a gardener as well! Others were far worse off than we are today as they were very poor and had no modern conveniences. We must do our best! Obviously, those who are organised will do better. If you have children, then as they get older it will become easier.

Together with your husband, work out responsibilities concerning the house and garden with the sharing out of chores. If you have children then develop some guidelines for their jobs, depending on their age.

I found it best to do one major chore each day. By the end of the week each room had one good clean. It is too tiring to do all the work in one day, unless of course you live in a small apartment and only launder for two!

Thankfully these days there is no longer the compelling urge to keep the house perfect. Women can waste a lot of time while their children are small, polishing floors.

I well remember when we laid our kitchen linoleum in our first new home. I polished that floor lovingly and was so proud of it. Unfortunately, the slightest scratch showed up, so I began demanding the children remove their shoes before they entered the house. I was always growling at them for forgetting to do this. Eventually sanity prevailed and I decided I'd rather have a happy family than a floor I could see my face in. Looking back now I think how ridiculous it all was and what a waste of time and effort. Especially as every six months or so I had to scrape off all the polish I had put on and then begin again.

Would you choose a 'too clean' home or a happy home? I chose to have a moderately clean, happy home!

How Much Work Should You Do in the Church?

And whatever you do, whether in word or deed, do it all in the name of the Lord Jesus, giving thanks to God the Father through him (Cl 3:17).

It is a good idea to sit down with your husband and talk over your church involvement quietly and objectively. The work you do will depend on your gifts and abilities, on whether you have children, on their age, if you do have them, and on whether you have a job outside the home.

Be realistic, don't try to do too much. Your first job is to care for your family, and to do your own work at home. If you have spare time and the energy, then you can do other things.

If you have a desire to add to the life and ministry of the church, but you have little children, then begin to prepare for the time when you can help. Study the word of God, cultivate your own spiritual life, encourage other young mothers. If you are older, and no longer have home responsibilities then work out your gifts, what you would like to do. If your gifts lie in the direction of community service, then it might be good to explore that option.

Old or young, keep learning, don't stagnate, keep advancing, read, listen to tapes, note down things that interest you. The kinds of things that interest you are likely to interest others and can become useful as illustrations later if you are able to teach or write.

Hospitality

Offer hospitality to one another without grumbling. Each one should use whatever gift he has received

*to serve others, faithfully administering God's grace
in its various forms (1 Pe.4:9-10 see also Ro.12:13).*

It is always good to have the beds made up and the room prepared before the arrival of visitors who are coming to stay with you. It makes them feel so welcome. One good idea I have seen is to keep a bowl of fruit in the visitor's bedroom.

Do think carefully before deciding to put your children out of their room for visiting ministry. If this is done too often it could cause bitterness to grow in their hearts, especially if they feel that they are continually put last, pushed around, and their lives disrupted.

If you don't have a room for visitors, then it might be good to find someone in the church who does, and who is able to take care of visiting ministry. Your speaker will need a decent bed to sleep in if he or she is to be rested enough to preach well.

In our numerous travels, sometimes our hosts have given us their very own bed, and we are always extremely well cared for. However, on one memorable occasion, many years ago, in a small country town we were given a camp stretcher. That was a very long night!

Remember too, a preacher who has given his whole heart in ministry can be very tired after a meeting and may need to be protected from enthusiastic saints!

Should You Have a Job Outside the Church?

There is a tendency now for pastors' wives to have their own career. In the USA there are some pastors' wives who even go to a different church from the one their husband is working in! I personally do not feel this is an option though I understand why it could happen.

I have recently been delighted to meet pastors' wives who have begun to use their talents in ways that take them out into the community and give them opportunities to meet and influence many different people; folk they would never have met had they stayed within their church walls. These talents include fine art, journalism, and operatic singing.

Nowadays it could be that the wife is the pastor and the husband who has his own career!

Some feel it is far better for the husband and wife to work together as a team, if that is at all possible. A good wife can be a wonderful asset to her husband, but we are all different and this is something that couples in ministry need to work out for themselves. However, it is true that if the wife is not there to work with her husband then he must find someone else to help with the work. If that someone else is a woman then there could be a danger of getting too close to each other, with all the peril that implies. There is enough danger facing a man of God, without looking for more!

Then again, for some women, it might be good to make some difference between herself and her husband's ministry. If she has that distance it might enable her to be more of a support to him, enabling her to minister to him more effectively.

Finally, you should come back to this: as a pastor's wife you should ask yourself, *"What do I feel is right and proper for me to do? What does God want me to do? What is right for my husband and for my children?"*

Have the courage to prayerfully consider the options and together with your husband strive to please God in everything you do.

Whether you go to work or not depends on many factors: training; the ages of your children; and finances. The ideal, if there are young children, is to be at home. It is a good idea to work out exactly how much you would really earn if all the extra costs of going to work were taken out. As a young mother you may find that working outside the home is not worth the enormous effort involved.

Should You Take in Foster Children or Boarders?

Father of the fatherless, a defender of widows is God in his holy dwelling. God sets the lonely in families ... (Ps 68:5-6a).

Because of the heart to minister in many pastors' wives, there is a tendency among them to take in foster children or boarders who need a home and some care.

In New South Wales (Australia) now the Welfare department do not advise couples to take in a child that is older than their youngest. The foster child could then influence the younger child, and if there is any problem this could have far reaching consequences.

If you have children of your own, they need to come first. They have been given to you by God; they are your first responsibility. Only when you are sure that all their needs are being met can you have time for another child.

Let the decision be a family one. Let your own children have a say in whether they can cope and review the situation at regular intervals. I speak here from experience as we did once take a foster child who was older by some years from our oldest child. At first it did not appear to affect our son but over a period of eighteen months he became increasingly stressed until we were advised by his school that we would have to release our foster child to take proper care of our own son. Our former foster child still remembers us with affection.

As far as adult boarders are concerned: When you take in an emotionally disturbed person you can no longer counsel him or her objectively. You become too close, too involved; part of the problem. They can lose respect for you. It is better to keep a certain distance when you are counseling people.

In the case of ordinary folk who need a home, remember your husband and children need their home to be a place of rest and refreshing. Can they have this with boarders in your home? How much of your time do the boarders take? Are you neglecting other important matters to cope with the boarder or boarders? Once again, I speak from experience. I tell my story in the next chapter of this book.

Chapter Three

Hallelujah! You're A Pastor's Wife.

(Lois Cronin & Alison Chant)

Lois Cronin is the wife of Mike, the pastor of South Eastern Christian Centre in Endeavour Hills, she is a dynamic speaker and a tremendous help to her husband as well as an inspiration to other pastors' wives in the Crusade. Lois has been preparing women for the task of pastor's wife for many years and graciously gave permission for me to use her material for this chapter.

Called and Chosen

Mark and Beryl were devastated. They had just been informed they were no longer wanted by their church! Three important families in the church had given them the news and they had no reason to disbelieve them. This had been Mark's first church and for three years he had worked hard and built the church to three times its former size. He and Beryl had poured all their love for God, their youthful enthusiasm, and their concern for God's people into their little church. Of course, they had made mistakes, but surely not that many!

That night they wept in each other's arms, and the next Sunday they resigned publicly from the church.

It was then they discovered the majority of the people wanted them to stay. People began to weep and beg them to remain as their pastors. They had not known of the decision to ask Mark and Beryl to leave. It was not a congregational decision, but the decision of the few families involved.

After seeking advice from their peers, Mark and Beryl felt

they should leave to keep the church united. If they stayed, the three families would leave and so, as they had already publicly resigned, they made the further decision to abide by that resignation for the sake of church unity.

As it happened, this couple went on to greater heights in ministry and God blessed them wonderfully. The church, after a few years of struggle, finally dissolved.

Despite the hard work and the spiritual burden, and sometimes the heart break that comes from ministry to the people of God, it is a privilege to be chosen to serve God's flock faithfully. Our reward is great, both here and in heaven. The costs are great too. However, as Mark and Beryl found, anything precious will be costly. We must endeavour to keep an eye on eternity, as the following scriptures attest.

> *I consider that our present sufferings are not worth comparing with the glory that will be revealed in us* (Ro 8:18).

> *For our light and momentary troubles are achieving for us an eternal glory that far outweighs them all. So we fix our eyes not on what is seen, but on what is unseen. For what is seen is temporary, but what is unseen is eternal (2 Co 4:17-18).*

> *Therefore, I endure everything for the sake of the elect, that they too may obtain the salvation that is in Christ Jesus, with eternal glory (2 Ti 2:10).*

As pastors' wives we are called and chosen by God for the task he has given us, just as our husbands are called to the ministry. Depending on the ability and gifts given to us by God, we may have a public or a private ministry. Either way, we are called to be help-meets to our husbands. In the words of Jesus,

> *You did not choose me, but I chose you to go and bear fruit - fruit that will last. Then the Father will*

give you whatever you ask in my name (Jn 15:16).

And as Paul admonishes us all, God calls ordinary people and makes them extra-ordinary:

Brothers, think of what you were when you were called. Not many of you were wise by human standards; not many were influential; not many were of noble birth. But God chose the foolish things of the world to shame the wise; God chose the weak things of the world to shame the strong. He chose the lowly things of this world and the despised things - and the things that are not - to nullify the things that are, so that no one may boast before him. It is because of him that you are in Christ Jesus, who has become for us wisdom from God- that is, our righteousness, holiness and redemption. Therefore, as it is written, 'Let him who boasts boast in the Lord' (1 Co 1:26-31).

A Special Grace

We are each given a special grace to carry out our task. We could not do anything without God's help and his enabling power. Remember Paul's words to Timothy,

God has saved us and called us to a holy life - not because of anything we have done but because of his own purpose and grace. This grace was given us in Christ Jesus before the beginning of time (2 Ti 1:9).

Your husband's call is your call too. You are one flesh and God calls you to respond to the work he has given you. However, some feel they need their own call and we respect that. Heather Eaton, who gives her testimony further on in this book, was called at an early age, and knew she was to be a pastor's wife years before she met her husband Dean.

From earliest times God declared us one flesh with our

husband,

> *The man said, 'This is now bone of my bones and flesh of my flesh; she shall be called 'woman', for she was taken out of man. For this reason, a man will leave his father and mother and be united to his wife, and they will become one flesh (Ge 2:23-24).*

God is our Master and Lord. Who are we to question his call? It is for us to obey and trust him to give us all the gifts and abilities we need to mould us into the shape he wants us to take.

According to Isaiah's stern admonition we must learn to trust God's working in our lives.

> *Woe to him who quarrels with his Maker, to him who is but a potsherd among the potsherds on the ground. Does the clay say to the potter, 'What are you making?' Does your work say, 'He has no hands' (Is 45:9).*

God will not give us a burden greater than we can bear. He helps us in our infirmities, and in our weaknesses. If we put ourselves into his hands, and allow him, by our obedience, to mould us into vessels of honour, we will be equal to the task. We don't have to be reluctant to follow his call. We must respond to it with all our hearts, and with an expectant faith that he will keep his promise to us. Jesus has revealed to us the test of our love and he urges us to trust him.

> *This is love for God: to obey his commands. And his commands are not burdensome, for everyone born of God has overcome the world. This is the victory that has overcome the world, even our faith (1Jn 5:3-4).*

> *Come to me, all you who are weary and burdened, and I will give you rest. Take my yoke upon you and learn from me, for I am gentle and humble in*

*heart, and you will find rest for your souls. For my
yoke is easy and my burden is light (Mt 11:28-30).*

We must find God's yoke and wear it. Then our attitude
should be to accept his call gladly and not chafe under it. If
we do strain against the call of God then his yoke will seem
hard, harsh, sharp and pressing.

Being a Pastor's Wife

> Being a pastor's wife is the most hazardous and
> dangerous occupation a woman can have. [6]

Judith made her preparations methodically. She is a tidy
person. She finished her work and then looked around. All
was in order; she could go ahead. She opened the oven door
and prepared to switch on the gas.

Sadly, she thought over the last few months. She could stand
no more - the angry words, the coldness, the unreasonable
attitudes. She wanted peace, an end to the conflict. This was
the best solution that she knew.

If only she knew why Paul and Beth had turned against her.
From the time she and Ray had taken the little family in a
year ago, they had all lived in harmony; but now for no
apparent reason Paul and Beth had turned against her and
Ray. After all they had done for them, it was devastating. She
could bear it no longer; she was too deeply hurt to want to go
on living.

She reached out to turn on the gas - and at that moment the
front door-bell rang....

Judith's life was saved by God's perfect timing. A dear friend
arrived in time to avert a tragedy.

You may say, *"This could not happen to a pastor's wife."* But
it can and has. By their very nature some people are 'loving

---

6 Marion T. Nelson, Christian Psychiatrist

and giving'. This pastor's wife, and many others, are full of compassion and take people into their homes and into their hearts. They are living out their understanding of what it means to follow Jesus. When the very people they seek to help turn against them it can be a very bitter trial.

In Judith's case it transpired that another member of her church had told some lies to Paul and Beth which turned them against her. Later the truth was revealed, and there was a reconciliation. Judith received an apology from all concerned.

Why do these things happen in churches? Why are some people so far from understanding the principles of Christianity?

You may say, *"I would never allow anyone to hurt me in that way."*

Maybe you would not, you may have a different temperament from Judith, being more assertive, and sure of yourself. Judith needed to be taught how to cope with these kinds of people and these different situations. If she had, she would not have been so vulnerable; which brings me back to the reason for writing this book...

She has now been taught, and she will not have to face this overwhelming heartbreak again. Next time, if there is a next time, she will be well able to withstand an attack of that nature.

Pastors' wives need to know that people, because of their own hurts and insecurities, can be cruel. These people need to be handled with love and compassion, they also need to be shown their wrong-doing and to repent of it, thus enabling them to grow into a greater understanding of the principles of living the Christian life.

I was talking with a very new pastor's wife recently and her cry was, *"Why didn't someone warn me of these things. If only I had been warned I could have been prepared, and that would have made it so much easier."*

This has been the cry of many young pastors' wives over the last few years and slowly the need is being met. More and more psychologists and counsellors are becoming aware of the struggles of the pastor's wife and the reasons for them. Mature pastors' wives are also becoming aware of the need to help one another, and to teach and prepare those who are just beginning to serve God in this way.

Two for the Price of One

Most churches expect two for the price of one. In other words, they expect the pastor's wife to fill the *"empty spaces"* in the ongoing life of the church. They expect her to be the receptionist, the tea lady, office worker, children's worker, and telephone counselor, without any remuneration.

And, because the pastor's wife, especially if she is young and enthusiastic, feels called by God to stand by her husband and do things for the Lord, she may neglect her own family life to "fill the gap". There must be a balance between family and church.

Karen was excited at the thought of the new church she and her husband had been called to pastor. The people were so friendly and helpful, and she was sure they would all get on well together.

She noticed that there was a job which needed to be done, so she volunteered. The next week she noticed another that needed doing, and so took that on as well. Without realising it, over the next few weeks she took on six jobs. They all needed doing and she was able to do them, so she did. After some months of working for the church as well as looking after her husband and children, she began to feel worn out. She couldn't get everything done; there seemed no time to relax. Every evening except one was taken up with church work. The children began to complain that she was too busy to give them the attention they needed, her husband asked her to rethink her position. She did and resigned from all but one of her positions.

Afterwards she said, *"It was all so stupid, I should have realised, but the jobs came one at a time and each one involved only a few hours per week. What I didn't realise was the accumulation of time they would take. Now other people have taken up the slack, I have more time for my young family, my husband is happier, and all is well."*

This is a mistake made by many enthusiastic pastors' wives. The task is there, it needs to be done, so they do it, forgetting that their primary role is to look after their husband and children and to keep their home a place of peace and happiness. A place where their husband and children can be refreshed and restored and made fit to face their world.

A Task Not Given by God

I made this mistake one year. It all began so innocently. A dear friend of ours, a widow, died leaving two teenagers. One was old enough to go into the army and had plans to do that, but the other one had another year to go at high school. He didn't want to move to a different school for his last year, so we took him in. This would have been quite within my capabilities and worked well for a time; but then an older brother asked if he could stay with us for a while, and then two more teenagers asked for temporary accommodation for different reasons.

Finally, I finished up with five boarders plus three of my own children who were still quite young, and a very tolerant husband. He kept saying, *"Are you sure you can manage all these people? Isn't it too much for you?"*

I was enjoying myself; it was fun having all of them!

It was a year later I noticed my knees were getting stiff. Usually at the end of a prayer meeting it was hard to get up from a kneeling position. Over the next few weeks I was reduced to crawling around the floors to do the vacuuming. I visited my Doctor and he examined me, and then asked what my lifestyle was. I told him I was a pastor's wife and that I had five boarders plus three children at home. He looked at me and said these words. I have not forgotten them, for they seemed to me to be a direct word from God.

"Mrs Chant", he said, *"If God had wanted you to have eight children, he would have given you eight children. Go home and tell your boarders to find somewhere else to live."*

I did, and they did! My knees improved and I have had no more trouble with them.

I was advised to put God first, take good care of myself, my husband and children; afterwards if I had time and energy, I could do something for the church. It does no good for the pastor's wife to be doing church work to the detriment of her primary task, given to her by God: to be a wife and mother.

People can have very strange ideas about their pastor.

One young pastor was found grocery shopping with his wife and children. His parishioner was greatly astonished and said, *"Pastor, you shop!"*

"Yes", answered the pastor, *"I also eat!"*

The pastor can get very absorbed in the life of the church, to the neglect of his wife and children. Balance is the word to keep you both on track. Stop and evaluate. Think! It does no good to save others if it means losing your own family. That cannot be a good witness and has happened far too many times in the past.

There may be some in the church who feel that because they are contributing to the pastor's salary, he belongs to them so he should be available when they need him. Others are more thoughtful. It is hard as a pastor's wife not to feel resentful when people demand your husband's time as their right. It is your right gently but firmly to remind them the pastor has many demands on his time, and they are only one of many. He will do what he can as God enables him. They should not expect any more than that.

A Double Standard

I have observed this anomaly: If the wife is the pastor, and her husband is the one in the role of helper, then a double standard is at once apparent. Instead of expecting the husband to be useful to the church in any way, the people are pathetically grateful if he does anything at all. Praise and gratitude are the order of the day. The pastor's husband is even praised for attending a meeting, and if he brings a dish to a potluck the people are overwhelmed. He is treated like a king! If the male pastor's wife was treated this way, there would always be a happy and contented spouse in the manse!

On the Other Hand

Pastors' wives feel they need to be four people in one! A good wife to her husband, thus freeing him as much as possible for ministry, and a good mother, even though coping with lack of time, strength and resources. She is also expected to be a good housekeeper; and finally, a good church member, attending all meetings and taking an active role. And all this while under the magnifying glass of the congregation's expectations of what a pastor's family should be!

She must cope also with living on a reduced income, receiving criticism from all sides, little appreciation or help, and feeling that her life is being lived in a gold-fish bowl! Little wonder some pastors' wives grow weary in well-doing!

Especially when her husband is expected to be available day and night, and when he tries to fulfil these expectations because of his strong call to help and assist others. The result can be burn out and bitterness for the family because they have had their legitimate needs ignored.

But there are some rewards. Listen to these words from Hebrews.

> God is not unjust; he will not forget your work and the love you have shown him as you have helped his people and continue to help them (He 6:10).

God does not forget you. A pastor's wife is blessed with a godly husband who is motivated to help others and see their lives turned around, a husband who desires always to do God's will in his life. One who is polite and gentle to his wife and a good and loving father to their family.

Her children are growing up in a godly home in the very best climate of love and security. Because of his flexible hours their father can spend valuable time with them. They are learning to discipline their lives and share with others; watching their parents witness to the unsaved and seeing them give unselfish service to God and the church. They are exposed to other godly people when visiting ministry is invited in, and they learn to meet new people and thus learn social skills.

The pastor's wife also benefits in other ways. She gets to travel to conferences, to visit other churches, to make wonderful friends. She has an outlet in the church to use her abilities. She meets many different and interesting people and has an easy entrance into the society of the city or town in which they live. She often receives generous gifts. She has the joy of seeing people come to the Lord and of helping them mature in Christ

Know Yourself

The pastor's wife needs to assess her talents, her abilities, and her weaknesses. This will help her to fit into her church role consistent with the way the Lord has designed her. This can be a trial and error undertaking. Be prepared to try any task you feel fitted for. You may surprise yourself! As Paul says in 1 Corinthians,

There are different kinds of gifts, but the same Spirit. There are different kinds of service, but the same Lord. There are different kinds of working, but the same God works all of them in all men (1Co 12:4-6; see also verses 7, 12, 18 & 27).

In many churches now there is no stereotyped role of the pastor's wife. A diversity of gifts is recognized. If you are in a small church, you may have to do some things that are not in your *"gift"* but you can train others gradually to take up these tasks until you can be released into your particular gift.

At any time, you may need to fill a gap, so you should avoid having the attitude that, *"I can't do that, it is not my gift."*

Three General Roles We May Typify

As a pastor's wife you are first a helper for your husband, but after that you may take one of the following roles.

Partner

In this role you may have a public ministry, you may counsel with your husband, visit with him; sing duets with him. This kind of team ministry can be very rewarding and enriching to a couple. In fact, in some circles this kind of thing is expected.

In this role you need to be aware of the danger of feeling so absorbed in your husband's ministry that you are losing your own identity. You may need some space to be yourself.

If you cannot define your own role in life, if you become a cipher, just a part of your husband's ministry, then you can become miserable and frustrated. If on the other hand you have a career and yet are unable to fulfil that career or find employment in that field, then you can feel trapped and unhappy. These reactions will in turn affect your husband and his ministry.

Enabler

You could be an enabler, actively supporting him from the sidelines but not having a public ministry yourself. The reasons could be lack of desire, small children to care for, an aged parent to look after, full time work outside the home - things that may limit your involvement.

The danger here could come from using your tasks as an excuse not to do the things that involve ministry, when the real reason is that you fear failure, or criticism. On the other hand, it could be that you see yourself only in a supportive role and there is nothing wrong with that. Either way don't allow inferiority to dominate your life. Rise up to take the risk of being involved. If you are not involved in the life of the church, you will not understand the pressures and demands your husband faces. You will see only your own needs and the needs of your home. If this is so you will become a further source of strain to your husband.

Specialist

If you specialise in one area you may be working in a different sphere from your husband. In this case the danger could come from growing apart by going in two diverse directions. This could be overcome if the two of you share your various realms by communication. This could then become very enriching to you both.

Over the years, as the needs of the home change and the children grow, your role will change; but whatever your role, it must be consistent with that of all pastors' wives. It is important to show wholehearted support for your husband.

The Hebrew word for helpmeet found in Genesis is 'neged', meaning 'counterpart' or 'the opposite part'. For psychological strength the pastor will lean on his wife. Emotionally any man is very dependent on the encouragement and support of his wife.

It is important too for the pastor to be aware that his wife is also one of his congregation and needs instruction and motivation. Opportunities need to be given for her to grow and develop spiritually. Not by coercion, but by encouragement and example.

During our life together I have always supported my husband, but he in his turn has also encouraged me to grow and develop my own talents. As soon as our children were grown, he made it possible for me to study, and to begin to teach in Bible College, a role I enjoy very much.

To some degree then, we may cover all three roles: we may be a partner, an enabler, or a specialist, however usually one of these three will predominate.

Our Priorities – Toward God

In the end God wants true worshippers, those who will worship him in spirit and in truth. Jesus emphasised this in his conversation with the Samaritan woman of John's gospel:

> *Yet a time is coming and has now come when the true worshippers will worship the Father in spirit and truth, for they are the kind of worshippers the Father seeks. God is Spirit, and his worshippers must worship in spirit and in truth (Jn 4:23-24).*

We have to be constantly watchful to spend time with God. We must not allow ourselves to become Martha's rather than Mary's. We need to cherish our first love (cf.Lu.10:39-42 & Re.2:1-7).

The Old Testament shows that the people of Israel had three main divisions: Warriors; Priests; and Levites. Those divisions represented warfare, worship, and service. All are needed; but notice that worship is central to the other two. If we lack worship, we will overbalance toward warfare or service. This will result in us doing warfare or service in our own strength and wearing ourselves out. This would not be pleasing to the Lord.

Remember Jesus appointed his disciples, first and foremost, to be with him (Mk.3:14-15).

To maintain our freshness and vitality, to be hearing from God; we must spend time fellowshipping with him. The most difficult time in our lives to maintain this fellowship is when our children are small. Usually it is not possible to spend large amounts of time in reading the Word and in prayer. However, we can still be turning our minds toward God during the time we are doing repetitive type chores, for we are told in Colossians that whatever we do it is for God, no matter how mundane.

> *Whatever you do, work at it with all your heart, as working for the Lord, not for men, since you know that you will receive an inheritance from the Lord as a reward. It is the Lord Christ you are serving (Cl 3:23-24).*

Our Priorities – Toward Ourselves

Once again, the word of God clarifies that we need to esteem ourselves on the foundation of our love for him and for others.

> *... Love the Lord your God with all your heart and with all your soul and with all your mind. This is the first and greatest commandment. And the second is like it: Love your neighbour as yourself (Mt 22:37-39).*

If we have not come to the place where we can accept ourselves and know we are precious and worthwhile in God's eyes we will have many problems as a pastor's wife.

Very likely we will be hurt, shattered, touchy, threatened, jealous, fearful, discouraged or depressed. We will be crippled by criticism, reacting with defensiveness, anger, aggression, or withdrawal. We will perform to be accepted and approved and will react with anger and hurt if we aren't appreciated. We will be possessive of our own domain. We won't be able to accept talented people who seem better than we are. We will be looking for negatives in others or be negative about ourselves. We will be anxious, fear failure and disapproval, and we may reveal perfectionist standards. Our relationships with other people are only as strong as our relationship with God. And the degree by which we love and accept ourselves will be the degree we love and accept others.

Personal Habits

We must be impeccable in our standards of hygiene. Our dress should always be neat, clean, and becoming. An easy-care hairstyle is preferable, so we may always be ready for any emergency.

I will not forget the time a distraught mother came to our home for comfort. She had just been told that her seemingly healthy baby was going to die of a crippling disease. I was in the middle of the washing and had my hair in curlers, I certainly wasn't ready for any emergency! When my husband came looking for me to help him comfort this poor little mother I demurred for a moment as I felt embarrassed about my appearance. My husband rebuked me for caring about something so trivial as my hair and clothing at a time like that and I had to agree with him. As if those things mattered at such a time. I quickly made myself tidy and sought to bring what comfort I could. After that time, I made sure I was always prepared.

We prayed earnestly for this family and, praise God, although this little one did eventually die, and although the family had been told that all their children would be afflicted in this way; God afterwards gave them two perfectly normal children.

Exercise, rest, and recreation are the hard ones. We can get so busy that we stop caring for ourselves. We hardly have time to think, let alone plan times of rest and refreshing. If our husbands are equally harried; then the problem becomes more horrendous. If you have young children, they can be of help here. At least while the children are younger, we must take time for trips to the zoo, picnics at the beach, hikes, bike riding, or lunch at one of the fast food outlets, depending on your tastes and the things you enjoy doing.

Mental Habits

Learn to acknowledge your feelings without letting them dominate you. Don't ignore them either. They need to be dealt with. Our feelings are governed by our thinking. If we can change the way we think then we can control or redirect our feelings. Unless there is some medical reason, such as an imbalance of hormones, we can learn to think in a godly fashion. We will then reap the benefits of walking in the revelation and understanding of who we are in Christ, rather than walking in our own strength, and reaping confusion and bad feelings.

We may wonder why we sometimes feel angry and frustrate-ed. This is always linked to what we are thinking concerning a person or a situation. Negative feelings about someone can be a warning to us to check our thinking about that person. We must take responsibility for our thoughts and feelings. We may not be able to control other people's actions, but we can control our own attitude, and our reaction to those actions.

If we try to change our feelings without changing our think-ing, we are doomed to failure. We can confess our anger as sin, however, unless we deal with our thinking concerning the event that made us angry, the feelings of anger won't go away.

We need to control our feelings and not be victims of them.

It is for freedom that Christ has set us free. Stand

*firm, then, and do not let yourselves be burdened
again by a yoke of slavery...So I say, live by the
Spirit, and you will not gratify the desires of the
sinful nature. For the sinful nature desires what is
contrary to the Spirit, and the Spirit what is
contrary to the sinful nature. They are in conflict
with each other, so that you do not do what you
want. But if you are led by the Spirit, you are not
under law (Ga 5:1, 16-18).*

Be aware also of pre-menstrual tension. Our hormones can
really affect our emotions. Watch out for self-pity during
these times.

Feelings and Communication

Pick suitable times and places to share your feelings with
your husband. Just before a meeting or while he is busy
preparing a message may not be wise! Don't drop hints; be
specific. If you are tired and need help with the children,
then tell your husband clearly. Men are different from
women! They prefer plain speaking. They are used to precise
instruction and detailed information. Their thinking is more
analytical and critical than the average woman's. It just
frustrates a man if his wife drops hints and then, when he
doesn't respond, blows up and cries all over him. Sometimes
we feel no one appreciates us; we give and give, and only
receive criticism in return. We begin to feel, *"Who needs
this? Why should I have every one's problems? I have
enough of my own!"*

Sometimes we feel like running away!

It helps to remember that there are other professions, which
require similar sacrifices from the wife. Think about the
wives of politicians, business executives, soldiers, sailors,
airmen and the like. They do it for an earthly reward; our
rewards are eternal, as Paul explains in Colossians.

Whatever you do, work at it with all your heart, as

*working for the Lord, not for men, since you know
that you will receive an inheritance from the Lord
as a reward. It is the Lord Christ you are serving
(Cl 3:23-24)*

We can turn a negative (lonely hours by ourselves) into a
positive, by using those hours constructively and creatively.
We can take up a hobby, we can sew, knit, listen to tapes,
complete a Bible Study Course. We can seek to know God in
our loneliness.

We must learn to admit that we are human; we are not
superwomen. God is still working on us. We must learn to be
patient with ourselves, not expecting perfection until the
resurrection! We should balance our Christian lives, allowing
God to work his will in us as Paul taught in Philippians.

*Therefore, my dear friends, as you have always
obeyed - not only in my presence, but now much
more in my absence - continue to work out your
salvation with fear and trembling, for it is God who
works in you to will and to act according to his
good purpose (Ph 2:12-13).*

Indeed, we show our strength and maturity when we can
reveal ourselves as we really are. It is reassuring to others to
know that we too face grief, and pain, and struggles. We
don't have to share personal details; but we can allow people
to see that we need their support and prayer. We don't have
to know all the answers. We aren't perfect. However, there is
no need for us to explode all the time either!

God does not share his glory; so, don't let people idealise
you; be real!

Our spiritual walk will have times of rapid growth and then
times of standing still, even slipping back a little. Sometimes
God will ask something we aren't ready for and he may need
to bring us around again until we are ready and willing to
step into the next phase of growth.

You can't please everyone so don't even try! You can't do everything people want you to do or be everything they want you to be. Learn to say, *"No!"* when necessary.

Avoid Resentment

Should nots" and *"ought nots"* bring expectations which, if they are not met, cause resentment.

- We put it on our husbands: "He should be more attentive to me."
- We put it on our children: "They should be an example to the assembly."
- We put it on the assembly: "They ought to consider our personal lives."

In this way we make our lives miserable with resentment, and with its twin, bitterness.

Learn to deal with failure, both in yourself and in your husband. When it comes, don't say, *"I told you so; I warned you."* He doesn't need to be told. He is already feeling badly enough. Instead be loving and kind, and warm toward him sexually, for this reaffirms your belief in him and his belief in himself.

"At least my wife loves me, I can't be such a failure after all", will be his reaction.

Develop a positive mentality toward failure. Just because we have failed doesn't mean we are failures.

> The man who does things makes many mistakes, but he doesn't make the biggest mistake of all - doing nothing. [7]

> Behold the turtle - he makes progress only when he sticks his neck out. [8]

---

[7] Benjamin Franklin

[8] James Bryant Coront

It's better to do something imperfectly than to do nothing perfectly. 9

A reporter asked Edison, the inventor of the light bulb, *"How do you feel about 10,000 failures?"* He answered, *"I've learnt 10,000 ways in which it doesn't work."*

I never see failure as failure, but only as the opportunity to develop my sense of humour.

I never see failure as failure but only as an opportunity to develop my understanding of God and develop myself.

I see failure as a necessary part of my walk in God.

You should learn from failure, and therefore not need to repeat it. A failure can be a stepping-stone, or a stumbling block. In Philippians the apostle Paul inspires us to look up continually, and reach out eagerly, for the prize God has promised us. We should not look back but forward.

> *Not that I have already obtained all this, or have already been made perfect, but I press on to take hold of that for which Christ Jesus took hold of me. Brothers, I do not consider myself yet to have taken hold of it. But one thing I do: forgetting what is behind and straining toward what is ahead, I press on towards the goal to win the prize for which God has called me heavenwards in Christ Jesus. All of us who are mature should take such a view of things. And if on some point you think differently, that too God will make clear to you. Only let us live up to what we have already attained (Ph 3:12-16).*

Learn to apply the blood of Jesus, as John tells us,

> *If we confess our sins, he is faithful and just, and will forgive us our sins and purify us from all unrighteousness (1 Jn 1:9).*

---

9 Robert Schuller

Resist condemnation! Know your position in Christ and where your righteousness is based. We have been justified.

> *Therefore, since we have been justified through faith, we have peace with God through our Lord Jesus Christ (Ro 5:1)*

We must deal ruthlessly with any self-pity that we might feel. We are told instead to,

> *Rejoice in the Lord always. I will say it again: Rejoice! Let your gentleness be evident to all. The Lord is near. Do not be anxious about anything, but in everything, by prayer and petition, with thanksgiving, present your requests to God. And the peace of God, which transcends all understanding, will guard your hearts and your minds in Christ Jesus (Ph 4:4-7; see also 1Th 5:16-19; Ro 8:28).*

A Martyr's Attitude

Do you have a martyr's attitude? Let us examine ourselves regularly and change any attitudes that need to be changed. We need to learn a hard lesson in life. We can't live other people's lives for them. We can't change anyone; only God can do that!

Here is an example of handling expectations.

"It would be wonderful if my husband was more attentive to me".

The truth is I can share how I feel, but I can't force a response from him. I can be responsible in my behaviour toward him, but I can't control how he behaves toward me, unless I try to manipulate him! Resentment can arise sometimes because we feel we own our husbands. We must surrender him to God. We must not feel, *"He's mine! He belongs to me. This is my time."* No, rather yield your rights to the Lord. You will find that as you surrender your rights, God will arrange circumstances to give you all the time you need with your husband. When the pressure of your demands is released, he will be happy to be with you and draw much strength from you to help him in his work.

Some women expect far too much from their husbands. They expect him to fill a place only God can fill. They drain their husbands until they feel they must withdraw. Don't be like that; rather be a fountain of refreshment, as you draw your strength from God; then let it flow to your husband (Pr 11:24-25; Re 22:12; Ge 15:1).

Times of crisis or the demands of some urgent need can occur that disrupt what we have planned. Unless we place our rights to our husband on the cross, we will become resentful and angry.

Goals and Desires

You should clearly understand the distinction between a goal and a desire. If you know how these two differ from each other, you will save yourself from much stress and frustration. A goal is the purpose to which I am unalterably committed, and for which I assume responsibility. This must be something which I can accomplish, and which is well within my control.

Never assume responsibility for a goal that you cannot control!

A desire on the other hand is something I want to happen but cannot by my own efforts make happen. For example, my desire may be for an unsaved relative to come to Christ, but I cannot make it happen. If we turn desires into goals, we will end up angry and resentful. We should pray for our desires, and work on our goals.

Here is an example: circle either G=goal or D=desire to indicate which one describes each of the following state-ments -

- G/D *"I want you to listen to me"*

- G/D *"I want the church to grow"*
- G/D *"I want to go to bed early tonight"*
- G/D *"I want to speak to my neighbour about Jesus"*
- G/D *"I want to be at church on time on Sunday"*
- G/D *"I want you to be encouraged by my friend-ship"*
- G/D *"I want my husband to rest on his day off next week"*
- G/D *"I want my children to love the Lord"* [10]

Delight yourself in the Lord and he will give you the desires of your heart. Commit your way to the Lord; trust in him and he will do this (Ps 37:4-5).

We should pray for our desires and work at our goals. Sometimes our goals must become desires. For an example if we have a flat tyre on the way to church our goal, to arrive early, must give way to a desire that we won't be late!

Remember this great saying,

> God grant me the serenity to accept the things I cannot change, courage to change the things I can, and the wisdom to know the difference.

True and False Guilt

We must learn the difference between the two feelings of guilt. Have you sinned? Then deal with it, put it under the blood of Jesus, and turn away from it, looking to Jesus who is the Author and the Finisher of our faith. He has broken the power of sin; he has destroyed the root of sin in our lives. We no longer are compelled to sin; we are free to choose to live a godly life in Christ.

False guilt comes from our own insecurities or over-sensitivity, but God knows our hearts.

---

[10] See Larry Crabb's *Encouragement* Bibliography.

This then is how we know that we belong to the truth, and how we set our hearts at rest in his presence whenever our hearts condemn us. For God is greater than our hearts, and he knows everything. Dear friends, if our hearts do not condemn us, we have confidence before God and receive from him anything we ask, because we obey his commands and do what pleases him (1Jn 3:19-22).

We can feel guilty for example -

- After legitimately saying, *"No"*, to someone.
- After failing our own standards.
- After failing others' standards.
- When we feel we must keep working.
- When we feel we could have done more.

Guilt leads people to act inconsistently. Then they over-compensate. So, a pastor's wife, feeling that her children are being deprived because of her involvement in ministry, may wrongfully indulge them in some other way.

Remember: you will never do anything perfectly, so allow yourself grace. God has poured out his grace for you! Whether you suffer from true or false guilt, Christ's death on the cross is your only solution. We cannot by ourselves live up to the standards of God, or even our own standards.

> Christ not only bridged the gap between God's holiness and man's sinfulness, he also bridged the gap between our own demands and our actual performance. In other words, through Christ we are made acceptable to God, and through Christ we are made acceptable to ourselves. If God can accept us, surely, we can learn to love ourselves. If God can forgive us, we can forgive ourselves. That's why guilt

feelings should have no place in the Christian life. [11]

Beware of Jealousy

Place me like a seal over your heart, like a seal over your arm; for love is as strong as death, its jealousy unyielding as the grave (Ca 8:6).

The other woman! Some men of high repute in our day have wrecked their ministries and their homes because they allowed their eyes to stray to another. There are different kinds of such women in the church.

There is the woman who looks for a strong, masculine, confident father image. She feels that, because he is a pastor, he is safe!

There is the woman who wants a surrogate husband. Many women, having no husband, or having an unsaved husband, dream a little of someone strong, dependable, a gentleman, courteous and kind. As they only see the pastor at stated times, they get an idealized view of him and this fosters a liking which is harmless enough; so long as the pastor is careful, and his wife is watchful.

There is the woman who merely appreciates the shepherding role of a man of God.

Then there is the woman who deliberately designs to lure a pastor into sin. She is not a Christian but only a pretend Christian who delights in destroying a leader of the people of God.

How can you guard your man? Work at your marriage, keep each other happy, contented, and at rest; fully satisfied with your home and family life. If you do this; then you will have a good basis for trust in each other. You are his greatest protection (after the Lord) and he is yours.

---

[11] Bruce Narramore; *You're Someone Special.*

If there is an American Cadillac in the garage, then who needs a German Volkswagen off the street!

Strategies for Handling Women of Misplaced Intentions.

Make friends with them. They will feel less able to approach your husband if you are showing them love and friendship. Don't withdraw from your husband physically when the woman is around. Stay nearby, stand next to your husband, do not allow her to make you feel like an intruder. Let her see your oneness, your unity, the fact that you are one flesh with your husband. We can claim this promise from the book of Isaiah,

> *No weapon forged against you will prevail (Is 54:17a).*

Because of the fall of some prominent ministries some wives feel insecure about their husbands. Because of their insecurity they displace this feeling on to their husbands and begin to feel afraid for them. On the other hand, it may be the wife is the one who feels vulnerable, and afraid that she can be tempted, and she may displace that fear onto her husband.

Don't expect your husband to explain his every move to you. He needs the stimulation that comes from his associates, even if one of them is a woman! We can't meet all his needs. We must trust God for our marriage!

A wife may also feel jealousy when her husband is constantly being called on, and she is in the shadows. The phone calls are always for him; he is the one people look to. His ministry is recognized and appreciated and hers is perhaps ignored. We need to give all those feelings to God and let him deal with them. If we are willing for him to deal with them, he will!

Have a Servant Heart

Jesus is our example in all things, he was not too proud to wash the feet of his disciples, and he calls us to follow in his steps. He reveals to us this vital principle:

> I tell you the truth, unless an ear of wheat falls to the ground and dies, it remains only a single seed. But if it dies, it produces many seeds. The man who loves his life will lose it, while the man who hates his life in this world will keep it for eternal life. Whoever serves me must follow me; and where I am, my servant also will be. My Father will honour the one who serves me (Jn 12:24-26; see also Mk 10:45; Ph 2:5-8).

Jesus' service came out of his authority. He knew God had given all things into his hand. He knew that he had come from God; that he was called and chosen by God, and he knew that he was to go back to God. He was perfectly secure in himself; he didn't have to defend his position. His importance didn't have to be proved (Jn 13:1-17).

We can take a lesson from this. If someone criticizes you, don't brood over it. If it is valid then change; if it is not valid then ignore it. Who are you striving to please? Is it not God?

One lesson we must learn. We cannot please all the people all the time! Therefore, we must work to please God. Then we can be sure we are doing the right thing.

As time goes by and we gain maturity, criticism will hurt us less and less. We will be intent on pleasing God, and all our circumstances will come into order as he guides and directs. Don't react to criticism by giving back the same as you receive.

What should you do when people come to you with criticisms of your husband? Here is one strategy: tell them that if they have anything to say, they can say it to him themselves. Men tend to be emotionally less vulnerable than women. Don't be trapped into passing on comments. They will find it easier to say it to you than to face your husband. Don't let them take advantage of you.

Be careful both of pride and of inferiority. Don't compare either yourself or your husband with others. There may be pastors with a more mature ministry or with different gifts. Comparisons are odious. Don't compare your families with other families, for the same reason. Everyone is different, and it is not fair to compare. It only brings discontent and envy and hinders our development and our husband's also. Those who make such 'odious comparisons,' show a lack of trust in God and in their lives. He does not want us all to be alike. He has different tasks for each one. Different places need different strategies, different types of people, and different gifts. Be content with who you are and allow God to mould you according to his will.

Chapter Four

Communication in Marriage

(Moya Enright)

Moya Enright and her husband Graeme trained with the Salvation Army and served God for some years with that denomination. Moya is a warm, bubbly personality and a dynamic preacher with a special desire to teach young mothers. She and Graeme have four lovely daughters Sharon, Priscilla, Christie, and Naomi. They now pastor Living Faith Fellowship in St. Agnes in South Australia .

Honest Communication

Communication in marriage is not a new subject for the '90's. For many years bad communication has been a major ingredient in the breakdown of many marriages.

Open honest communication is essential in any relationship, how much more so for a pastor and his wife. They are after all to be examples to the flock. The most crucial relationship in any local church is the relationship between the pastor and his wife.

Our churches must see a couple of genuine people who have learnt to live happily together in this life. Not two plastic people, pretending to have it all together.

Most couples enter marriage with great hopes, and desires for a wonderful future of joyful harmony. Unfortunately, many of the dreams and expectations are idealistic and unreal.

We spend months during courtship convincing our loved one how wonderful we are, and how we desire to meet their every need. We are selfless in our love, giving all, demanding little.

We choose to overlook some of those irritating little idiosyncrasies, calling them cute. We are oblivious to the underlying motivation behind our efforts - not so much to love, as to be loved.

Too little time is spent in discussing the real issues of a marriage relationship. Neither partner has a real understanding of what the other is truly expecting of them. Fanciful ideals and expectations create a rather wobbly threshold over which to carry the new bride.

Entering the Ministry

Many enter ministry together in a similar fashion. Full of zeal, enthusiasm, hopes, desires, and expectations, many of which are unreal and unfair. It is so easy to rush into ministry without a clear definition of what you are working towards, or why and how you are going to do it.

What begins as a committed partnership, to win the world and feed the flock of God, can somehow turn in on itself and begin to crumble. Many go on for years living far below God's intended joy for them: not understanding the destructive dynamics that are in place.

Expectations and Disappointments

How many young pastors' wives have been disappointed to find they are not married to a Billy Graham, or a Paul Yongi Cho, after all! And how many young pastors have been discouraged to find his young wife is not a dynamic Catherine Booth, or a Katherine Kuhlman.

Open honest communication with our spouse can save us from the snare of disillusionment and help us discern the real person from the phantom. A profitable exercise for any couple in ministry would be for both husband and wife to make separate lists of what they feel defines the role of, 1) The pastor, and 2) The pastor's wife.

Allow plenty of time to think it through thoroughly. Next

comes the fun part of comparing lists. (This will need to be done when each are feeling reasonably amicable of course).

There will undoubtedly be conflicting ideas presented but, if done honestly it will expose some of the unreal, and unfair, expectations we impose on one another - and ourselves. It should also highlight any priorities which have slipped to a lesser place. Be frank and honest about every area.

Now, work together on a fair and customized profile for both this particular pastor, and this particular pastor's wife. Be prepared to alter priorities - to add or subtract some things and highlight areas which need to be compensated for by team members. You can then pray together about these things.

As the profile of the church and your family changes, so the roles may need to be adjusted. This should be discussed periodically, to ensure each is aware just what the other is expecting of them, and to guard against any potential pitfalls.

Feminism and the New Generation

This generation we serve, with our husbands, has not existed before. There are new concepts in society which have affected men, women and children. The feminist movement of the 70's has had a drastic affect on the local church. The world has been thrown upside down through the results of male/female role reversals and church women have become insecure and confused about their roles. This has affected many pastors' wives.

I was raised in a denomination where women took equal training and rank with men. Even now, they have a higher ratio of women in full time ministry than men. It was nothing new to me for women to take the lead. This was never a competitive thing with the men. There was never any need for debate on women's rights in the area of ministry. It was the natural outcome of any life, called and equipped. The simple fact is that much of the ministry - missions, social, and church work, would be defunct were it not for the women responding to the call.

Entering the ministry in the early 70's as a single female pastor, I then went on to marry and, jointly with my husband, served in our first local church. The hullabaloo of the women's liberation movement seemed insensible to me. I was already liberated through Jesus, as were several generations before me. I felt the feminists didn't know what they were talking about.

However, it is sad for me to look back now, and see the devastation, and ruin, that has been caused by that movement in our society. The saddest thing is to see the subtle and insidious way the philosophies of this movement have crept into church life over two decades. They have eaten away at the very core of our existence and family life.

So now, while on the one hand I have no question at all about the validity of women fulfilling a ministry role, I would give this advice; to younger women in particular. Take time in the early years of marriage to work on excelling as a wife and mother. Establish your marriage on solid ground. Don't be deceived by the world's opinion that you need to be performing in some ministry role to be accepted as the wife of a pastor.

Career Pressure

It's my opinion that families in our churches need to be set free from the pressure on women to find a career outside the home - or even within the church. A pastor's wife who is happy to be at home is a great example, and a release for other Christian women. This doesn't mean that a woman, pastor's wife or not, can't pursue other interests and goals, but these should never be looked upon as the source of her true value.

Pastors' wives; don't abdicate your chosen role of wife and mother. Learn early to discern between vision and ambition.

There is plenty of time and scope for ministry, but don't neglect your family for it.

Working as a pastor is a vocation, and not merely a career. It has nothing to do with ladder climbing or brownie points, but everything to do with listening to the Father. A ministry in the church can be a great asset in a pastor's wife, but it can also be a great stumbling block, for herself and her husband, if ambition and striving are in her heart.

If I were starting out again, I hope I would take my own advice seriously. I hope I would relax in my own gifts and sit back awhile and allow my husband to find his own level. If a wife doesn't try to force her husband to perform well in ministry then he will mature as a pastor far more quickly. Having him secure in his role is a good foundation on which a wife can then venture out into some area of ministry. Overall, a happy and contented pastor means a happy and contented pastor's wife.

Wisdom and Encouragement

My main role as a pastor's wife is to keep my husband happy and encouraged, and to assist in any way which becomes necessary, while we go through different phases of church and family life. Sometimes that means helping with the workload, and sometimes it means backing off.

I think I've learned to trust my husband's ability to lead the congregation. I realise he will do just as well without God's little helper. I hope I reflect that to the women in our church. It is amazing; the way God equips a saint for service if we give him half a chance.

Books on Communication

There are many well written books on communication in marriage. I suggest working your way through one of these WITH your husband, and then develop some good communication principles. While we can each learn independently, it's surprising how differently a husband and wife can interpret the same piece of information. Our perspectives are very dissimilar. Reading these books alone does not benefit as much as studying them together and discussing chapters as you go. You will be far more likely to implement good ideas and principles you discover if you read the books together.

Most husbands need to be told very clearly what their wife's limitations, abilities, and needs are. No matter how many hints are dropped, subtle, or unsubtle, he will most likely miss them. Don't be cryptic or talk in riddles. Be clear precise open and honest.

Limitations

The things a young wife can keep pace with before the babies arrive is often very different from what she can accomplish with two or three little ones at her ankles. Don't be afraid to acknowledge limitations. They are not evil. There will be plenty of time later for more spiritual things.

Communicate clearly about your physical, spiritual, and emotional limitations at any given time. Don't allow room for resentment to grow: 1) From you toward him because he won't ease the pressure, or 2) from him towards you because he doesn't understand the reason for your lost zeal.

Practicalities

Communicate clearly about practical things; like the need for a regular clothing allowance for yourself. (If he wants to project a good image of himself, you need to be seen to be well cared for). Keep him informed about the increasing costs of living; just talking about these simple things will ease the load for you.

Don't feel obliged to protect your husband from the added pressure of these everyday areas. If they are a source of anxiety or depression to you, share them with him. They are his responsibility. He has broad shoulders. You are not helping yourself, or your husband, if you keep these worries from him. The fact that he is a pastor does not remove the fact that he is your protector and provider. Keeping him in touch with the pressures of everyday living will also keep him in touch with the real world that his flock lives in.

Pastors in general could use some good clear advice on the needs of their wives. Many don't know the pressure put on their wives by the expectations of the people. Many do not have a clear understanding of their wives' role. Perhaps one of the great Christian men writers could include a chapter on these matters in a book for men in leadership.

Sharing with Others

Informal fellowship and sharing times with other pastors' wives are very beneficial as long as everyone is prepared to be fairly transparent and real. There is much to be learned from pastors' wives who have 'walked the road'. There is also great encouragement gained from shared experiences.

Pastors' wives in general could do with a pretty good dose of encouragement, self esteem, and confidence. This would allow them freedom to be themselves. The unreachable intangible image of the pastor's wife should be toppled from its pedestal - both in the minds of the people and in the understanding of the pastors' wives themselves.

The Importance of Your Own Confession

Of all the people we communicate with, we talk to ourselves the most. Be aware of, and also beware of, your inner conversations. Watch how you talk to yourself! Sometimes it is good to toss things around in your head, but it can also be a destructive activity. We can go over an incident so many times in our minds, arguing from this side and that, by the time we actually discuss things with our husbands we have blown it out of proportion - all in our own minds. Be careful to keep your inner reasoning factual and honest, whether you are talking about yourself, or others.

The advice of the apostle Paul (2 Co 10:3-5) not to allow any high thing to exalt itself over the knowledge of Christ in my life, has been a constant help to me. I remind myself to call into subjection the many vain imaginations of my heart and weigh them up against the flawless mirror of the Word of God. How many problems I make for myself by neglecting to do this! Learn to discern the imagination from the fact. Don't react to vain imaginations - act upon the truth.

Helpful Book:

Joanna & Allister McGrath, *The Dilemma of Self-esteem*; Crossway 1992.

Chapter Five

Some Personal Testimonies

Joan Beard is now a widow, her husband Bill has gone to be with the Lord, but Joan remains an integral part of the large church in Wollongong that was founded by her husband. She and Bill began in ministry in 1954, the same year that Ken and I were married and began our ministry. Joan has some wonderful stories to tell of their pioneering days, and I know you will be thrilled to read of their experiences of many years ago.

Early Days - Joan Beard's Story

Our First Ministry

My husband and I were in ministry for more than forty years. Just after we were married, we went to live in Leeton NSW, on an Aboriginal reserve called Wattle Hill. We had both decided that we should serve the Lord full time, live by faith, and trust in the Lord for all our needs. Bill and I believed the Lord had called us to minister to the Aborigines in the area.

Dangerous Times

Our home was a large caravan, which we shared with Bill's brother Cliff, his wife Helen, and their first child, Sharon. We had some wonderful times with the precious people at Wattle Hill. Many came to know the Lord, and had their lives completely changed. However, there were some very scary times also. Often at night, and in the early hours of the morning we heard fights and beatings in progress. Once we watched in horror as a man produced a carving knife to stab a pregnant woman. Fortunately, the woman was saved by an old lady's quick action; she grabbed the knife out of the offender's hand. She was a brave lady, braver than we were, we just stood there frozen to the spot.

God's Provision

We experienced some interesting times. Our physical needs were met, and food was provided. Sometimes we would find a box of groceries on our doorstep. At other times, as I went visiting, the lady of the house would give me the gift of a carrot; at the next house I would receive a parsnip or a single bunch of celery. By the time I reached home I would have enough vegetables to make a pot of soup for dinner. We ate a lot of vegetable soup! Another provision for our table was through Bill and Cliff catching rabbits. We ate rabbits stewed, baked, boiled and cooked in a variety of other ways.

Paddy Melon Jam

A sense of humour was essential for those pioneering days. The Leeton cannery gave us their frost-bitten oranges; we would eat so many oranges that Bill and Cliff would say they tasted like pineapples as a joke. Once when the cupboard was bare Bill and Cliff were invited out for a meal. While they were gone I decided to go out for a walk and I found a melon growing in a paddock. Thinking it was a jam melon I took it home and proceeded to make some jam with the last of the sugar we had. After cooking it I was appalled at its bitter and terrible taste. I found later that I had used a paddy melon, which was poisonous, and all the jam had to be thrown out.

When Bill arrived home later that day he had heard about the jam. Kindly he said, "*Never mind, I have brought you home something to eat.*" From his pocket he then produced a piece of lamb's fry, wrapped in a tissue. He had taken it from his plate while no one was looking and slipped it into his pocket. I appreciated that little morsel, and Bill's thought-fulness. We lost a lot of weight in those days, but we certainly didn't starve to death.

God Continues to Provide

The Lord was so faithful to us during this time even though we did some unwise things. I remember the time we ran out of petrol. We were in our big mobile caravan on the way to a crusade meeting. There we were, stranded, with about an hour before the meeting was due to start, when along came a man in a little German Volkswagen. He stopped, and asked us who we were, and what we were doing. We found out that he was a Christian and would come to the meeting that night. He was just about to drive off in his car when he came back, and said, "*The Lord has just told me to give you my tithe money*! We said, "*Thank you very much*!" Rejoicing, we went and put petrol in the caravan, and arrived at the meeting on time.

God Knew I Was Having a Girl

A special memory for me was when I was expecting my first baby. I desperately needed some wool to make some baby clothes. I prayed and asked the Lord to supply my need. Not long after this I received a large parcel in the post. I opened it and there were twenty balls of pink wool. I knitted three layettes with it, hoping I would not have a boy. Of course, God knew ahead of time that I was having a girl. That was precious to me; to think that God would use a lady, from my hometown, to send me wool for my baby.

Our first missionary journey to Leeton was certainly a time of learning, testing, and blessing. We left there after two years to go north. "Wattle Hill" was never the same again; even the police testified to this, as they claimed they were seldom from this time called on to break up fights on the "Hill".

In the early days of our ministry we moved all over the country (just ask our two eldest daughters, they still complain about it). We were certainly pioneers in those days, starting churches here and there across the country, doing many weird and wonderful things, going through many painful experiences and trials, as well as much learning and blessings.

We have been able to pass on our many learning experiences to others, so that they might be saved from making the same mistakes we did. I am so pleased to say we have been in Wollongong for twenty-four years now. The Lord led us from Campbelltown (by a series of miracles) in 1969, to start a church in Wollongong. We have seen it grow from a small home fellowship into a beautiful prosperous and growing church, from which many ministries have gone out all over Australia.

I have appreciated being able to settle down, as it was very hard moving all the time with small children. We have four beautiful children, and we thank God for each of them. They are so precious to us, as are our sons, and daughters-in-law and our nine lovely grandchildren.

Most of the responsibility of bringing up the children was mine, while Bill did his pastoral work. I could not get involved with church work too much during that time. I believed my children were four very important people who needed to be cared for and brought up to know the Lord. As the children grew, I was able to become more involved in the ministry. They don't stay small for very long! Now that they have all married and have left home, I can be a fulltime pastor's wife, lady's leader, and musician.

I have travelled with Bill around Australia and also overseas on several occasions. On the whole I love being in the ministry and being a pastor's wife, being able to serve the Lord and the body of Christ. I thank God for his faithfulness to us. He is always there in the good times and the hard times. All glory and praise belongs to him.

Another Testimony

Heather Eaton is a delightful lady. She lives in Adelaide with her husband, Dean. Their son and two daughters are all grown, and Heather has completed her University studies and taken up the job of Librarian for Tabor College, Adelaide. Heather, like many of us who began in the ministry at a very young age, has learned through her experiences. I'm sure you will enjoy her testimony, and some of you will empathise with her over her trials.

The Call of God

I was married at nineteen and within a week my husband and I found ourselves in our first ministerial appointment. We had left the city to move to a church in a country town of 25,000 people. Our faces were shining with anticipation for what we had been called to do. The stipend was only $50.00 a week, but we were keen to live by faith. The people accepted us, and the senior minister and his wife were wonderful to work with, showing great patience in all their dealings with us.

My Lack of Training

Dean and I were so idealistic; nothing could stop us fulfilling God's call on our life. My husband had been to Bible College, but I had no training whatsoever. That didn't seem to matter as older Christian women gave me their gems of advice!

Your calling is your enabling; your availability is better than ability; and don't wear trousers, makeup, or earrings.

My! How things have changed since then!

Disillusion and Depression

God did many wonderful things during those first three years, including giving us two children to love. Yet I had become a victim of my own cynical heart, which led me to experience months of deep depression. I could not see myself surviving another week in the ministry let alone another forty years. Why had this happened?

"*No*", the devil had not led a landslide attack on my person, and "*No*", he had not completely separated me from God; although I'm sure he was quite pleased I was temporarily in the injured category. The bitterness that was eating me away came from within. As people began to disappoint me, my idealism began to diminish. It was replaced by cynicism and depression. Maybe youth and inexperience had caused this, yet how are we to grow up into wisdom without pain? My own zeal diminished with financial hardship; the Lord always provided enough for our needs, but I coveted more. Criticism aimed at me was not taken in grace but defended against. All this was the beginning of my education about people and me.

People Skills Lacking

I would get myself tied up in knots over people. *"Why won't they change and let God work in their lives? Why are they venting their anger on me? What have I done?"* I'd only tried to help!

In the end I would get angry to the point of being consumed in my own private tirades. Then the Lord spoke to me from his Word.

"These shall not enter the Kingdom of heaven .... robbers, liars ... "

"Yes, that's right Lord," I agreed.

But then I read ... *"outburst of anger"*. I was pierced to the heart and rebuked by the Lord as conviction gripped me.

My Weakness Became God's Strength

Through all the dark times I can see that my weaknesses in the flesh led me to a place of total despair; but it was there that the strength of God could work in my life. He never gave up on me. Whenever I needed him most, he would come in all his strength and power to heal, forgive, and love me.

People's expectations of their pastor and his wife can be so daunting that they can immobilise them in the ministry. Before I entered the ministry with my husband I was under the illusion that a pastor's wife must always be joyous, bouncing around the church, spreading goodwill, looking immaculate. She must never be tired, she must sing like an angel, play the piano like Dino, be constantly feeding the church freeloaders. She must also have a perfect marriage, impeccably behaved children, be always smiling (even at 2 a.m. when someone decides to drop in), run the Sunday School and the ladies meeting, preach, lead worship, and so on. Of course, I could never match up.

If anyone knows a woman who can do all those things, or if anyone thinks they can do them all then please let me know!

Shattering the Illusions

We must shatter the illusion of our congregation concerning the myth of the pastor's wife. As a young pastor's wife with small children, whenever I met someone half resembling the above I would feel absolutely useless. At these times I would go back to what God had called me to do, instead of trying to keep pace with others.

I soon became very protective of my role as a wife and mother, knowing that the years of childhood with my young ones would pass quickly and that I must foster my family life with all my energies. Our first mission field is our children.

The reality of life in most cases for ministers' wives is that they will suffer financial hardship, stress to the maximum, a husband who often shows tendencies to become a work-aholic with a Messiah complex, an uncertain future (you can never say to your children, *"Yes! we are going to live in this house for a long time"),* unreal expectations from people, followed by their criticisms. There is often pressure on a pastor's wife to be another pastor. I have resisted this temptation, put on me by others, as I know God has not led me to do this.

Counseling Others

Women would cry on my shoulder about their marriages. One lady said to me, "*It's alright for you, you are married to Dean. You can't possibly understand.*"

I do have a good marriage, and can honestly say my husband is my best friend; but it hasn't always been easy living with someone who, for great lengths of time, is only seen in the house between the hours of midnight and 8 a.m.

Another woman was giving me a great tirade about her husband who ended with, "*And he never mows the lawn.*"

I thought that was normal for husbands!

Women complain to me about their husband's lack of attention, yet at times I feel the same lack, because everyone thinks they own my husband.

Dean and I both learned after a time that our relationship with God, each other, and our children, was the number one priority in our lives. We can cope with most things if we are secure in each other's love.

This concept led to a retraining process for the congregation. The church had to learn that there is a cutting-off point, a sacred circle of the family, and no one crosses over that line. Christ requires a sacrifice of us, but there are some sacrifices he doesn't require, yet the church can demand them. We must discern the difference between what God requires and what he does not require, if we are to go on in the ministry.

Many Changes

Things have changed in the last twenty years. Many pastors' wives work out of financial necessity. Should she enjoy that work and make a career of it? Or should she enjoy making a career out of being a mother and a housewife? Should she have a life of her own?

While the church looks inward, gazing at its own navel, how are we as the body of Christ to spread the Gospel to all the world? Let's be open to God doing things differently from the way he has done them before. Sometimes we shut up the best assets of the church within its walls and won't let them out. If a pastor's wife must work, let her enjoy it without feeling guilty about it. You never know, she may turn out to be an effective witness as she keeps in touch with the real world. I have learned that I need to be myself and not an impersonation of someone else. Having outside interests, that have nothing to do with the church or my husband's work, has been a wonderful blessing which has enriched my life with my family.

Transparency

The transparency expected in the ministry is often painful. You open your heart to others, as you are either empathising with them or in need yourself. Then something you have said is taken out of context and gossiped all over town. You become wary the next time and appear less open, and then people say you are cold. You can't win!

Some are disappointed in your performance.

"The last pastor's wife was on five committees and per-formed several different tasks."

When this was said to me, I thought about it, then it dawned on me that the previous pastor's wife was in her late fifties, no longer with small children, and without a part-time job.

Some others are surprisingly encouraging. As I met one lady for the first time she exclaimed, *"Oh! You're the new pastor's wife. You are nothing like I expected!"*

When asked what she expected she replied, *"Oh! You know, boring, sensible shoes, and a bad perm."*

Criticism

One of the hardest lessons I have come to learn is the real reason why criticism is aimed at my husband. Of course, the devil enjoys this process of disunity. When people aim their anger at the pastor it is really God they are angry with. God hasn't delivered for them, but they see instead that it is the pastor who hasn't helped them. Their problem isn't with the pastor, it is with God, and that is where they must go to resolve their personal difficulty.

People also have a habit of transferring their own guilt onto you. At one time a person who was a very clever and manipulative man convinced us that our marriage was in trouble and so were the marriages of many of our friends. While we were analysing where we had gone wrong, it was revealed that this man was actually having an affair. To cover his own tracks he had taken our attention from him, and turned it onto ourselves. An interesting tactic!

Pressure

The pressure on our family life is at times intense, yet this is all the more reason to make the effort to spend time with our children. Often this means getting out of our own home. People expect us to have angelic children, and some people do!

Mine, however, are three very strong-willed, loud extroverts that do not get swallowed up in a crowd but appear to be a crowd by themselves. The humiliation that comes from having your child removed from the Sunday School and brought back into church because he has just attempted to strangle another child cannot be described.

But this is reality. Kids get stressed too, and as parents we need to protect them, and remove as much of that stress as we can, not add to it.

Needless to say, my child did not go unpunished, as he had

to learn responsibility for his actions.

Advice

Try to keep the church away from the house as much as possible and don't talk about the bad things in front of your children, otherwise they could be the next generation of cynics.

Satisfaction from Being a Pastor's Wife

I still remember the day the Lord gave me a vision and called me to be a pastor's wife. My immediate reaction was to chastise myself for a vivid imagination; but the Lord persisted with me until I finally accepted what he was saying. I had no idea what lay ahead. I was seventeen at the time and had only been a Christian for eighteen months. I stored this vision in my heart and waited for the Lord. Now fourteen years later I have been living in that calling for twenty years.

In many ways the life of a pastor's wife is inglorious, but the paradox is that I know I would be miserable outside of the ministry. How do I know?

We did take six months off at one stage, but the God-given desire for ministry would not go away. Instead it increased, and I was given a fresh revelation of God's love for the church.

In the ministry we see people at their worst, but also at their best. The glory and the joy of seeing people changed into the likeness of Christ are unsurpassed and so I praise God for the opportunity to be a pastor's wife.

From Pastor's Daughter to Pastor's Wife

Sharon Jones is the wife of David, a busy pastor currently working in a Christian City Church in Bargara Beach. Queensland. Sharon is currently writing a book on her and David's experiences in fostering children. They have three sons and two foster daughters.

Conforming

I remember the first Sunday night my father allowed me to wear jeans to church. My mother was nervous about what the other women in the church might say. No matter what else is said, pastor's children are expected to behave and dress better than the other children in the church. In the 70's wearing jeans to church in the evening was bordering on the unacceptable, but they were new jeans and my father said, *"Why not?"* Why not indeed! If our children are praising God and living for him, let them wear jeans.

By the time I hit my late teens I remember distinctly receiving the impression from someone that after the good training I had growing up in a pastor's family I would make a perfect pastor's wife. *"No way,"* was my response. What woman in her right mind would want to share her husband with a congregation, to have him on call 24 hours a day 365 days a year; always having to be the first at church and the last to leave. Who wants to live up to a multitude of expectations knowing it is impossible to reach every one of them. Who wants to be the recipient of secrets, of confidentialities, and the burdens of fellow pastors. And last of all who wants to have very few close friends, none of them in the church, or to have every action and utterance exposed to public opinion. What a life that would be; at least that was my opinion at the time.

That was not the life for me, but I knew I wanted to serve God in some capacity, maybe as a missionary, where everything I did and said would be gratefully received. I thought that would be a great life, where I would be revered and honoured for my sacrifice. On the other hand, who needs church life, where you feel you need to work like a slave and this is received as an expected contribution.

Some Positives

Of course, there were positive moments in being a pastor's daughter. It meant you were close to the top of the heap; you had the ear of the boss, and you met people who moved in the first Christian circles. You had parents who followed the example of Jesus, and though they sometimes fell short at least they were trying.

Belonging to a pastor's family I knew what a sacrifice following that call to divine service entailed and instead I wanted to marry a rich man and live in the lap of luxury for the rest of my days. I didn't want to have to live by faith or wonder where my next cent was coming from. I didn't want to be dependent on a group of people and their tithes for my livelihood.

Unfortunately, as God sees it, no pain, means no gain! No persecution, no character, no sacrifice, no heavenly crown. You reap what you sow in and out of God's kingdom.

The Call of God

As I grew into maturity, I felt the call to divine service more and more strongly. I was 25 years of age when I finally gave up looking for a rich man and surrendered my life to God. His will finally became paramount in my life and then I met my future husband who had just prayed the same prayer.

David was a Youth Pastor, and I accepted my fate with good grace and took the yoke of divine service upon my shoulders knowing exactly what road I was about to take. It was to be one of sacrifice, and yet in God's eyes full of heavenly reward. Of course, if I could have done anything else and been happy I would have but when you are called it burns in you like a fire that cannot be quenched.

And being a pastor's wife is a life of sacrifice, let no one belittle you if you have chosen this path. Only another pastor's wife can empathise with you. We can accept this yoke of ours or continually buck against it and thereby destroy ourselves, our marriage, our husband's ministry, or at the very least settle for second best in God's eyes.

When our heavenly Father calls you to the life of a pastor's wife he has handpicked you for a special commission. He does not send you on a mission without equipping you for the task. I have found myself weary and burdened when I have fallen down in the areas of intimate prayer, times of one on one with the Father because it is; *"When you draw near to him he will draw near to you."* And if I have neglected times of reading the Word, *"My Word is a shield about you,"* And have forgotten to give thanks in everything, not 'for' but 'in.'

There will be times as a pastor's wife when people will hurt you, will denigrate your husband's ministry, and will try to tear down as quickly as you build up. But God will win the victory in every situation sooner or later. We all wish it to be sooner but God's timetable is not ours. He provides the task, he expects us to work the task through to completion.

Nothing can prepare you for being a pastor's wife. It is a daily experience where all you can do is lean on the Holy Spirit as comforter and teacher. Asking him to give you those words that will bring life and healing, and that will give you the wisdom to balance your roles as wife, mother, sister, and member of the congregation.

The Mission Field

Guard your children, they are truly your first mission field. Train up your child in the way he should go and he will not depart from it. I truly believe if we spend time helping our children establish a relationship with God that they will never seek fulfilment in the world. Teach your children about Jesus, read the Word to them each day. Pray with them over all their little troubles and give thanks for all the good things. They grow so quickly, be there for them, be the example of Jesus in their lives, don't let the demands of the church come between you and them. Be there for the running race, the fashion show, each one of their small triumphs. They will never forget if you fail to be the parents you should be. What a blessing and victory for God's Kingdom for people to see a family who loves God, who has joy in serving him, whose children love going to church and being part of building God's Kingdom. What a victory for God and what a blow to the devil.

Be encouraged to walk in your calling. Lean on the Holy Spirit for wisdom. Stay close to God and his Word, giving thanks always. God has called us to be living sacrifices not dead ones.

Chapter Six

Ministry Pressures in a Nutshell

(Liz Bailey)

These pages have been contributed by **Liz Bailey.** She and her husband Rob Bailey pastor Ballarat Christian Fellowship in Victoria. They have two adult sons, Bretlyn and Nathan. Liz is an experienced teacher, in both Government and Christian Schools, and is a widely read researcher. She is also a gifted communicator who has helped many find answers to everyday living.

With the help of their sons, Liz and Rob have held seven camps for pastors' children and have directly affected over 150 young people from these families. Our addendum on the advantages of and disadvantages of being a P.K. comes from their research. They recently helped to research a book by Cameron Lee, *"Helping P.K.'s Through Their Identity Crisis"*.

Here we have in note form the external and internal pressures of ministry.

How to Deal with Ministry Pressures

A. External Pressures.

1. The people you lead have an 'image' or 'ideal' that they expect you to fulfil.

1) So, you are pressured to be:

- Victorious
- Available
- Punctual
- Gracious

- Loving
- Wise
- Efficient
- Capable

2) And you are pressured to:

- Look like a pastor's wife
- Be present at everything
- Be a perfect wife, mother, and homemaker.

The Solution:

- Encourage your people (by relevant sermons, books, tapes, videos, prayer).
- To accept everyone as they are
- To resist putting expectations on anyone
- To let people be themselves
- To forgive others for their lacks and failures (1 Co 13:5 TLB)

2. Let them see some of your struggles on the way to victory. Admit your humanity, your failures.

You are pressured to do:

- Visitation
- Run lady's meetings
- Preach
- Song lead
- Choir
- Secretarial work
- Counsel
- Nurse
- Cook
- Babysit
- Welcome new people
- Hostess

- Remember all things

The Solution:

- Realise most people will still love you and respect you even when they see your mistakes.
- People will relate better and more naturally to you if you relax, be yourself (and make mistakes and apologise!).
- Learn to say 'No' or have a go! You might be great at it! You need to know your motivational gifts (Ro 12:6-8).
- Be thankful for all the benefits of being a pastor's wife.
- Don't try to juggle too many things!

3. Your husband may put high expectations upon you.

- Does he expect perfection?
- Does he compare you with others?
- Does he think you have a particular ministry (and you don't agree?)
- Does he feel threatened by you?
- Is he critical?
- Does he expect you to be tireless?
- Does he expect strict organisation, punctuality etc?
- Does he leave all the child training and house management to you?

The Solution:

- Communicate openly with him.
- Share your goals and desires.
- Admit your fears, inabilities, insecurities, lack of desire.
- Be prepared to work hard on those areas he wants you to excel in, after mutual agreement on your

capacity and potential.
- Be open to change; develop, grow, and mature.

4. Your peers may transmit certain attitudes to you.

Do they make you feel?

- Insecure
- Threatened
- Inadequate
- Fearful
- Jealous

The Solution:

- Recognise that this can be caused by THEIR feelings of inferiority, competitiveness etc.

B. Internal Pressures

1. Pressures you put on yourself create stress:

- I should be a witness in everything
- I should be perfect
- Every book, tape, sermon, video on my role makes me feel condemned, guilty, and inadequate
- I must hide my faults and failings
- I'll never be like 'her' so I'll never make it (or my husband will never make it)
- I must justify (or hide) any variations from the expected 'image' (e.g. outside employment, social activities).
- I should be able to song lead.

1) Many of these thoughts come from our feelings of:

- Inferiority
- Insecurity, Inadequacy
- Rejection
- Competitiveness

- Comparisons
- Fear of man (Pr 29:25)
- Pride

2) These need to be dealt with!

- By confession and repentance
- By healing of the subconscious
- By immersing yourself in the Word of God.

2. I must set a perfect example so others have a standard to aim for:

1) Be yourself!

- Accept yourself (Ep 1:6)
- We don't all have to be the same!
- You are unique! (Ps 139:13-17)
- You don't have to fit into a mould.
- You don't have to compare yourself! (2 Co 10:12)
- You don't have to compete with anyone! Ep.2:10).
- Release yourself!
- Forgive yourself!
- Take time to have fun
- There is no ideal, no image of what your role should be!
- Remember, poor attitudes and conflicting emotions tire you, e.g. resentment, unforgiveness (He 12:15; 3 Jn 2).
- If you try to maintain an image of perfection as a standard for others to reach they will only resent you, feel inadequate, threatened etc.

2) My children must be perfect.

- They need the same release to be themselves, not to have standards put on them.
- Don't have a separate set of rules because they are pastors' children.

- They need your love, time, attention, praise, physical contact etc.
- Emphasise the advantages of being the children of leaders.
- Be in control of your own life.

3) I must be available all the time.

- Teach people to make appointments.
- Don't allow yourself to be manipulated
- Learn to say 'No' without feeling guilty
- Remember no one is indispensable
- Delegate and trust others.
- Being a pastor's wife can be an ego trip!
- Remember, a pastor's wife is PART of who I am – not the WHOLE of me...and NOT my profession. It is dangerous to get all your status and satisfaction from being a 'pastor's wife'.

4) Take the time to have some fun. Learn the value of shutting off from the pressures (Mk 6:3) with:

- Hobbies
- Sport
- Music
- Fashion
- Friends
- Relatives
- Turn the phone off, take a nap
- Have an early night
- Have a family night
- Take a weekend off

5) Don't hang on to people's problems and crises or get emotionally involved (Mt 11:28).

What should you do when you can't handle criticism of yourself or criticism of your husband; when you get your hackles up, get on the defensive, refuse criticism or reject it?

The Solution:

- Learn to take it to the cross and die to self (Ga 5:20)
- Love and forgive the critic (Ep 4:31-32).
- Look at the criticisms objectively.
- Realise God is the one to please (Pr 29:25)

3. Pressures you put on your husband may be unrealistic.

- If you put pressure on your husband, you will find your own pressures increase.
- Trying to make him something he is not destroys him and you.
- Accept him AS HE IS.
- Don't compare him with other men, study motivational gifts (Ro 12:6-8) and ascension gift ministries (Ep 4:11).
- Study the temperaments together with your husband, work out your strengths and weaknesses.
- Put your ambitions on the altar. Don't idolise the ministry.

1) Your husband needs:

- Encouragement
- Support
- Praise
- Security
- Confidence

2) Your words are important to him – you can make or break your man (fragile "male ego"). Seek God to learn how to:

- Help him to handle criticism constructively.
- Help him to guard and protect his ministry.

- Prevent yourself from doing anything that hinders him from reaching his potential

Chapter Seven

The Missionary's Wife

(Jana Locke)

Jana Locke is serving the Lord with her husband on the mission field. They are working with the Church of England Mission in Pakistan and Jana was secretary to the Bishop until his retirement. As well as her wise words on counseling you will be moved to compassion by her testimony of what it means to be a missionary wife.

Women Missionaries

Women who have spent several years, or even much of their married life on the mission field, are a separate group of people who have, in many cases, undergone much privation.

The first question that should be asked is, *"Can anyone counsel these women?"* The answer is, *"Yes,* and, *No."* Many try, some doing more harm than good; but, interestingly, research has proved that friends and neighbours, in certain circumstances, can be as competent as professional counselors.

Basic Requirements for the Counselor

- The counselor should know the Lord Jesus personally, and have an ongoing walk with the Holy Spirit. A person who does not fulfil this basic requirement cannot hope to understand a missionary wife, or the spiritual dimension and commitment she has.
- The counselor needs to be part of a local church under the authority of his pastor or priest, from whom he in turn is fed, thus gaining wisdom and

insight.
- Some training in basic counseling is most valuable, though an untrained empathetic friend can be of immense value.
- A counselor needs compassion and caring that is non-smothering and non-possessive. A caring person displays it in his voice, his eyes, and in practical ways.
- The counselor needs the ability to see potential in all people; to see them as Jesus sees them.
- Above all he/she should be a good listener. Very few people realise how little they really listen to others. I have known one lass to gain a Psychology degree for a counseling career yet not have the ear, the empathy or the love to listen.

The Missionary Wife and Her Problems

"If she is trusting the Lord and drawing strength daily from him, surely she should be on top of things and living a life of victory?"

That is the sort of comment that comes from a person who has not been in the shoes of a missionary wife!

Christians are subject to the same maladies as non-Christians. Christ does not make us immune to them. Some reasons why missionary women have psychological problems, though they are born again and serving the Lord, include their genetic makeup, their environment, their over-all physical health and stress. Stress is the primary cause of both psychological and physiological problems.

Most of us are acquainted with people who suffer from depression, anxiety, phobias, and other psychosomatic disorders, which include migraine headaches, and on the mission field, the "runny tummy" syndrome. On the mission field women usually tend to mask their inability to cope with stress. It's OK to have malaria, or hepatitis, or typhoid, or even migraine headaches, but to admit to depression or anxiety problems is a sign of weakness, which results in a *"You've no right to be here"* attitude from co-workers. A "'runny tummy" too can always be blamed on Giardia, or Amoeba though it may be caused, not by one of these parasites, but by a stress condition.

One missionary admitted he knew where every toilet was in every airport in the country. He was admitting to a fear of flying which upset his stomach. Most missionaries have a bout of Giardia which is debilitating, but so is a "stress tummy".

Specific Stresses for Missionary Women

Putting children into boarding school; an overworked husband; being overworked herself, due to many factors; lack of exercise and recreation; lack of close friends; lack of deep language; pressure of financial hardship; and religious oppression.

The Lord does help and strengthen us, but we are not overcomers all the time, we are still human. Counselors of women missionaries need some understanding of these things.

Putting Children into Boarding School

This is never an easy decision and is so often misunderstood by relatives, friends, and supporters at home. Children are seldom put into boarding to give their mother an easy time at home, so that she can concentrate on ministry and put that before her family. This would be very rare! Home schooling has many limitations – the longer we are here the more I become aware of those limitations through mothers who are endeavouring to do it.

It does not become easier as the years go by; to put children onto a train for a thousand-mile journey, or onto a plane if there is an airport close enough, and the money to pay for a ticket! The heartache, the tearing, continues through the years, but our love for the Lord continues. He bore scars for us, so we too bear scars.

One mother of four with her last just going into boarding school was finding it difficult to put "the baby" in, even though the child of six was very keen to go with the rest of the family and with other children from various parts of the country. As the mother was bemoaning her struggles, another mother (of one) reminded her that she had only one, and that one too had to go into boarding. It is never easy.

We have a wonderful Missionary school here in Pakistan which caters for both the American and the British systems of education. We are really blessed. Even our Australian children can graduate here from year twelve with British and American qualifications, and then gain entrance into an Australian University, usually with flying colours.

I remember the times when, after sending my three off to the train to travel one thousand miles from me, I cried my eyes out on the bed. I felt I had given all I had to the Lord. What more could he ask of a mother. Years later two of our children are many thousands of miles away back in Australia. It is a stress. Others have to cope with sending children to another country for their schooling.

Counselors need to understand it is love which impels mothers to put children into boarding. Love for Jesus, and love for the children, because they know it is the best place for them to be.

Overworked Husbands

I don't think I know more than one or two men on our field who are not overworked. Why do they allow it? Is it the male achievement syndrome? It could be in some cases, but mostly it is just that there are not enough hands or mouths here to do the job, and they work because they love.

The wife needs a commitment to the work, and the counselor

needs to understand this also. I was once told by a well-meaning counsellor that I should live in the city while my husband worked in the desert. What Christian counsellor would recommend that a missionary couple separate if they really understood the call of God?

Overworked Wives

Counselors at home don't understand that we cannot go to the supermarket and buy a trolley of goods and then just stack them in the cupboard at home. Firstly, there is no super-market in many places. Then there is the endless cleaning of grains to get stones and rat dung out of it, and the endless soaking of fruit and vegetables; the sterilising, or filtering, of water just to make it fit to drink. It depends where you live how the water comes! Ours came on the back of a camel for three years; out of a hand-pump well 100 yards away for two years; now we are blessed with water in a pipe.

It's these minor frustrations that become too great. Usually we cope with the big ones, such as changing location, but when a rat bit the toes of one of my sleeping children (eleven years) I felt I could no longer cope.

Many women have part-time or full-time jobs. Some are fortunate to have adequate house help, but not all. One runs a clinic for women and children from 7.00am - 2.00pm, then goes home to get lunch. By then she is too tired to cook and eat, after seven hours working in a humid climate with inadequate facilities and facing heart rending cases she cannot help or cope with!

Lack of Exercise and Recreation

In an Islamic culture we cannot take exercise as we would in our home countries. It would be ludicrous for a woman to jog or walk briskly. I know of a European woman who tried to ride a bicycle. It is just not cultural! She was knocked off and spat upon. As missionaries we cannot afford to use the swimming pools in the big International hotels in this country. A few years ago it was possible. Now it is just too expensive. We are not allowed to use the military one here in Peshawar as we may give the military Aids!

We need to be creative, but how? It is up to the individual. Different ones find different ways. Some find none. It is not helpful for the counselor to say, "*It's too difficult, God would not ask that of you.*"

Lack of Close Friends

Some are in locations where they are the only Europeans in town. Some can and do make close friends of the local people. This may sound a good idea, and it is good; but as we are from different cultures the local people can never understand how we think; and we can only try, by living with them, and reading all we can about their culture, to understand them. In Peshawar my closest friends are not Pakistanis, but Moslem Afghans who speak five languages and have degrees running out of their hands. Yet in Sindh, my closest was an illiterate Hindu prostitute with whom I could only just communicate.

Deep Language

Many of us can communicate in the local language enough to get by. Others, because of their greater knowledge of the language, can have a deeper ministry, and some can communicate at a very deep level. The latter is the most desirable, but for a wide range of reasons it cannot and does not happen. The counselor needs empathy to hear what the missionary woman is saying when she, "has no one to talk to".

Finances

We all need to trust the Lord to supply our needs. Sometimes he does supply, sometimes he shows us other ways to manage, and sometimes he doesn't. There are times when missionary families have to return to their home country, not because of a failure in health, or education, or a myriad of other reasons, but simply because their home support team cannot keep them any longer. The affluent west, with those who have no real knowledge of poverty, having Government employment, sickness benefits, unmarried mother's benefits, Aboriginal benefits, widow's benefits etc. do not know how to give.

Recently a British Christian research worker discovered that, over-all, Christian families give only 1% of their actual income to the Lord's work. Those who give the basic 10% tithe, and those who give well above it, are all outweighed by the majority who say they "cannot afford to give".

Religious Oppression

The threat of kidnapping is a constant thing. One colleague was recently kidnapped and later released. Others have given their lives for Christ.

Those are some of the stresses that missionary women succumb to. These stresses mostly result in wide ranging physical symptoms. It would be better if missionaries were better prepared and told what can happen to their bodies, and how to cope when they notice these symptoms. Better medical and psychological help could be taught to new missionaries. For example, a very basic fact is that Dettol and Savlon lose their power very shortly after opening, and in a little time are no longer effective. Betadine is the antiseptic to use, it treats more factors, and lasts much longer after opening. Too few of us are trained medicos and we learn these things too late.

So, how does a counselor cope with a missionary wife! I have listed a few things which need to be practised.

Listen, Listen, Listen

Listen, not only to the words and sentences a person uses, but also to the non-verbal signals that are given - the tone of the person's voice, the inflection, the speed. Are the sentences muddled or coherent? The facial expressions, bodily movements and dress are all vitally important. Good listeners watch as well as listen, for the body picks up and express emotional stress.

Empathy is another ingredient of good listening. Empathy is not the same as sympathy. Sympathy listens to another's pain and gives the response, *"Oh poor you, that is too much to bear!"* Empathy seeks not to feel the same as the person in pain, but rather to see the world through that person's eyes without becoming swamped by their troubles or pain. It is to walk with someone.

Confidentiality

Confidentiality is so important. The counselor must be careful not to share something about another woman missionary, because even if she is on a different field in a different country, she could be well-known to the missionary wife to whom the counselor is talking.

If the counselor is going to tape interviews, then the counselee should be told. It is shattering to the relationship for the counselee to find she has been taped without her knowledge. Confidence is broken and probably lost for good.

Acceptance

Acceptance of the person is vital. The quiet, shy, hesitant person who may have been squashed by circumstances and culture, and the person who can't stop talking and who seems so very extroverted - all are different, all need to be accepted just as they are, and loved unconditionally. Let the life of Jesus shine through you. Then, in time, the first will feel accepted and want to talk, and the other will stop the incessant talking. Paul Tillich says, *"the first duty of love is to listen!"*

Don't Lecture

A counsellor should pray with people; but don't lecture them by means of a lengthy prayer. The woman missionary doesn't need a lecture. She needs love and empathy, then prayer. Let Jesus into the situation. He can heal the hurts, though the scars may well remain, just like the scars Jesus bore for us in his hands and side.

Clarify

Ask simple questions. "*Do you mean ...* " or "*Are you saying ...*" Don't be afraid of silences. Learn to understand silences as much as speech. Listen to the language of tears. Like silence, tears can convey many different messages. There can be joy, pain, sorrow, frustration, and even anger. Sometimes the question can be asked, "*What are those tears trying to say ...?*"

This good listening requires the full attention of the counselor. Don't interrupt. A good listener will add, "*Can you tell me more about that?*" or, "*How did that feel?*"

We can all, even though we are not trained counselors, take courage and comfort in these words from John Powell in his book, *Will the Real Me Please Stand Up.*

> Most of us, when we are in the listener's role feel compelled to be speakers. We feel a compulsive inner urgency to interrupt others as soon as they start to reveal themselves. We feel a strange obligation to advise them, and to support our advice with a few chapters from our autobiographies. We jump in at the first pause and go on non-stop until we are exhausted and the other person in near despair. Regrettably, I have done this to others. I have also had this done to me. I have experienced the sadness of not being heard because someone had not cared enough to listen to my sharing and to learn who I really am.

Don't offer advice" writes Myra Chave-Jones in *The Gift of Helping*. Most people don't want it and will not use it. It is unhelpful to say, *"If I were you I would".* or *"I think you ought to"* ... because you are not me, and your view of what I ought to do is yours. The only real value of good advice is that it makes the person giving it feel better.

Avoid the trap of becoming a problem solver for the missionary woman. Better to say, *"I don't know what you should do. What do you think? What are the possibilities?"* The missionary woman is more than likely highly educated, though on the human level may not be able to use her qualifications and experiences to the full. Here is one last observation from John Powell.

In the role of the listener we should offer only suggestions and never directions.

He goes on to explain that adults are adults; not children; and must assume responsibility for their own behaviour and lives.

Gary Collins, in his book *How to be a People Helper*, says that effective listening should include five steps –

- Building a relationship.
- Exploring the problem.
- Deciding on a course of action.
- Stimulating action.
- Encouraging the person to apply what he has learned by launching out on his own.

Those are all applicable to counseling a missionary wife. Mr. Collins has looked at numerous accounts of Jesus' ministry and used that as a pattern.

First, he explains how, in Luke 24:14-15, we watch Jesus draw alongside the travellers who, from the way they turn the events of the past three nightmarish days over and over in their minds, still seem to be suffering from shock. Jesus takes the initiative and the trouble to establish a rapport with them so that they trust him. Having built up a relationship, Jesus goes on to explore with them the nature of their problem. Why were they so discouraged? Why were they so stunned? He seems to have listened attentively as they poured out their perplexing tale, giving them ample opportunity to air their frustrations, doubt and disappointments. Then having penetrated to the heart of the problem and under-stood it, Jesus decided on a course of action. With skilful use of questions and suggestions, Jesus sorts out the confusion by challenging their thinking and encouraging them to think differently about the string of curious events that precipitated their crisis of faith.

But far from keeping himself detached or aloof, he comes close to his fellow travellers and joins them for a meal. This fraternising was not an invitation to become dependent on him, however. On the contrary, we read that quite literally, Jesus vanishes from their sight. This disappearing act seems to have spurred them into action and, on their own initiative, the travellers head back for Jerusalem where they become encouragers of others." [12]

So, in summing up, many factors make a good counselor, but a person who hopes to counsel and help missionary women really needs to have "been there, done that" empathy.

---

[12]   J. Huggett *Listening to Others.*

Helpful Books

Joyce Huggett, *Listening to God;* plus *Listening to Others.*

John Powell, *Will the Real Me Please Stand Up.*

Myra Chave-Jones, *The Gift of Helping.*

Lawrence Crabb, *Understanding People.*

Michael Lawson, *Facing Anxiety- Stress.*

John White, *The Marks of Melancholy.*

Stan DeKoven, *On Belay.*

Gary Collins, *How to be a People Helper;* plus *Christian Counseling.*

Anne White, *Healing Adventure.*

And books to help missionary children:

Jill and Roger Dyer, *What makes Aussie Kids Tick;* plus *Scamps Scholars and Saints.*

M.K. Merimna, *Bees Make Honey.*

Chapter Eight

How to Be a Pastor's Wife and Like It!

(Vanessa Chant)

Vanessa Chant is a popular convention speaker and has been used in ministry, both here in Australia, and overseas in Singapore and Malaysia. She is the wife of Barry, currently pastoring Wesley International Church in Sydney, and the mother of three and the grandmother of twelve. She and Barry have been in ministry for 45 years. Vanessa has her Master's in counselling and is currently working on her doctoral thesis. All their children are following the Lord and active in ministry.

Difficulties and Dangers

How to be a Pastor's Wife and Like It is the title of a book I read a long time ago.

I remember one or two lines from it:

"Difficult people are sent across our path for our perfection."

On reflection I think one of the most difficult areas of ministry is criticism or coping with difficult people. Rarely do we change them, but when we encounter them, we learn a great deal about ourselves. Quite often it's not a pleasant revelation, yet Jesus told us clearly that whatever we do for the least of his brethren we do for him. Also, this opposite truth, that whatever we do NOT do for the least of his brethren we do NOT do for him (Mt 25:40 & 45).

After thirty years in ministry I am still sure of one thing; that is, I have been called to serve. Serving the Lord sounds so grand; but then comes the hard times -

- Moving from one church to another, or
- When a task you have been comfortable in is no longer required, or
- You have to move over for someone else who can do a task "better" than you can, or
- You have another child!

It is then you find there is a fine line between the desire to serve, and an attachment to the task. When the job is taken from you, sometimes it is a relief and sometimes it is hard.

For many pastor's families it is moving that is a difficult issue. Whenever we left a church, I left something of myself behind. I missed the friends and relationships that had built up over time. It takes valuable time and effort to establish new relationships.

There is loneliness in leadership, though if we trust him Jesus can keep us content.

> It is in that discovery that the key to a woman's identity lies. If women search for their identity in roles, they make idols of those roles, of their careers, their homes, their children or husbands. None of these things and none of these roles can give women what they are searching for. It is only on the narrow path up the mountain, only in a first-love relationship with Jesus Christ that a woman will find what she seeks. [13]

Larry Crabb in *The Marriage Builder* says much the same as Kari Malcolm. It is only when we have our relationship with our Lord the way it should be that we function best as Wife, Pastor's wife, and Mother. The times of greatest frustration

---

[13] Kari Torgeson Malcolm; *Women at the Crossroads,* IVP.

for me have been when I looked to my husband to fulfil for me those things only Jesus could accomplish.

One of my greatest challenges in ministry was when God called my husband out of local church work into a para-church ministry. We had waved the denominational flag very high, it seemed impossible to turn around. As I believe my husband's call is mine, and as I'm a slow learner, I accepted the fact that God was calling him into something different. My difficulty was that after twenty years I had begun to understand some of the complexities of local church work and my role in it, but I didn't understand where I fitted into the new vision. It took time, but I learnt finally through pain and joy to adjust. In some ways it's a lonelier road, but as I try to remain close to my Saviour, the way becomes clearer and clearer.

> *Whatever your hands find to do, do it with all your might, for in the grave, where you are going, there is neither working nor planning nor knowledge, nor wisdom (Ec 9:10)*

The freedom I have now (after more than thirty years in ministry) to work for the Lord, is perhaps the most exciting phase of all, yet perhaps the most dangerous. New opportunities are opening to me to minister in many places, to share experiences. There are also more opportunities for me to follow areas of interest that I have had on hold for a lifetime. There is the possibility that I could dash off in all directions at once, as time is passing and there is much I want to do and to achieve. This was made clear the other day as I was sharing with a pastor's wife who was feeling frustrated that her husband was always so busy. She is capable and wants to follow some of her own interests that have been impossible till now, especially as she has had a large family. I came away from talking to her with this deep impression: *"Yes, by all means do something, but with one proviso, keep the relationship between you and your husband a high priority."* For myself, I am enjoying my relationship with my husband more than I have ever done in my whole life. God is good.

I have enjoyed the role of pastor's wife. It is a great privilege to serve the Lord in his way, despite the difficulties. I have also become aware that many Christian professional people have the same pressures on them as they seek to serve God in their various roles.

Ministry and Family Life

Ministry is like marriage and family life, you wish that, with the knowledge you now possess, you could have another run through. I would love to mother my children over again; I've learnt so much. However, all we can do is to say, *"Sorry for the mistakes,"* and remember that we did try. I'm forever thankful for what God has done in the lives of my children. I can't help but shudder to remember those first few years in ministry. Thankfully, the grace of God was present, for despite our naiveté, God blessed.

Should God Always Come First?

The best book I have come across on the pastor's family is Marshall Shelley's *The Healthy Hectic Home – Raising a Family in the Midst of Ministry* [14]

Marshall Shelley asks several searching questions related to priorities in our lives that are very revealing:

- What does it mean to say God is first? How specifically do we put him first?
- Does that mean we should spend more hours alone with God than we spend with our family members?
- Are we serving God by doing God's work?
- If so, then is church work the way we put God first?
- Or is church work, "our career", a lower priority?

---

[14] Word 1988.

Shelley goes on to explore the situation further –

> Perhaps the greatest problem with the God first, family second, career third perspective is that real-life situations can't quite be so neatly arranged. Responsibilities simply can't line up first-second-third. At different times; when does God deserve my full attention? In practice priorities can't be stacked like blocks.

The problem with putting priorities in a list is that things on the end of the list seem unimportant, e.g. good works, and neighbourhood. Or as Shelley puts it *"... priorities can't be stacked like blocks."*

Criticism of this approach is rife. One criticism is that we now have "familiolatry" Another criticism is expressed in the magazine *Christianity Today* –

> For years it has been popular among evangelicals to list three lifetime priorities in this order: God, family and church. More blatantly, one evangelical family expert has written that 'family – next to God – is the most important and influential agent on earth'. In these popular rankings, family usurps the place the New Testament assigns to the church. [15]

After years of talking about this subject, I'm still learning; however, my husband and I have developed a diagram which has helped us. Here are our priorities, you might need to rule up yours differently. I hope you find this helpful. The other circle reminds us of the areas to consider.

---

[15]   Clapp Rodney; art. *Is the Christian Family Biblical,* Christianity Today, September 16th, 1988.

Sorting Priorities –

IF OVER COMMITTED
DELETE FRINGE ACTIVITIES FIRST

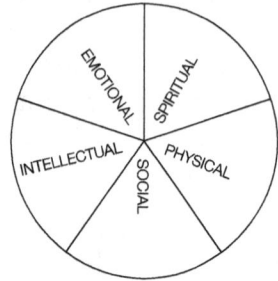

We have a circle with God in the Centre, for our relationship with our Creator influences all that we do. Then we have the priorities in our lives that we cannot change; partner, children, work, and church. As we move to the outside of the circle, we have the added responsibilities. If we are under stress in any area of our lives we need to work from the outside of the circle, culling what we can. We all must do this from time to time. In fact, this is a good exercise to do annually. This circle concept has helped many people.

For many people in ministry, the matter of our "calling" complicates our priorities. Sometimes we must make choices that are hard, but we make them because God has called us to this particular area. The simple drawing of a seesaw has helped me many times as I have had to choose between my family and my work. It has helped me to make some practical decisions.

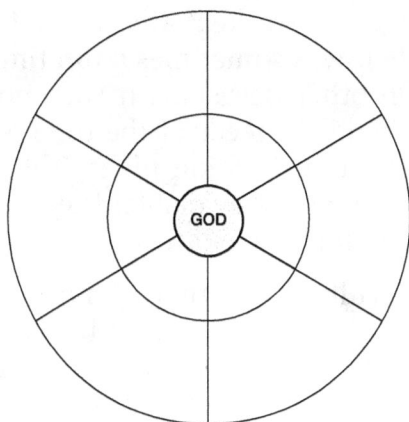

IF OVER COMMITTED
DELETE FRINGE ACTIVITIES FIRST

Family Night

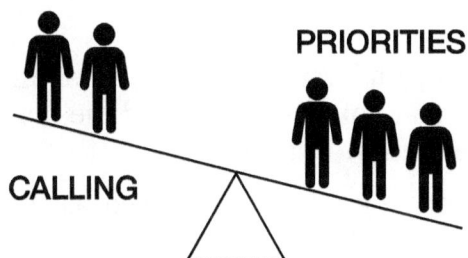

God has certainly blessed our family and for that I am very thankful. However, one simple strategy stands out for us and this might be helpful to pass on. It all began when we realised, we had been neglecting our children, sometimes for what seemed important. We asked God for creative ideas, and this is what he gave us –

For many years we had a family night once a week. It was marvellous for our family. It was a diary commitment, and, short of an emergency, we kept this night free. When the children were little it was sometimes a fun time, a time to go out for a treat. On other occasions it was more devotional, depending on the family's needs at the time. As the children grew it became a communication night. The children knew that this night we would be available; they could keep what they needed to share for this night.

There was one difficulty at this time in our lives; to find time for us as husband and wife. We read books by people like Robert Schuller, who had a date with his wife every week, and we longed to have that kind of time together. Now that our children are self-sufficient, we do enjoy our special night. If we are very busy, we can look forward to this! Planning for these occasions helps our relationship and is refreshing and strengthening. It was while sorting out our priorities that these ideas emerged.

Submission in the Home

Wives submit to your husbands as to the Lord! (Ep 5:22)

It may help us to understand this word 'submission' if we look back to the state of civilisation and the home during the time Paul wrote these words.

Women had been degraded and viewed as the property of their husbands for centuries. The wife was a drudge, a slave, or a toy of her husband, valued or despised, in the eyes of the community, according to the husband's desire, as she still is in some parts of the world.

Into this situation came the Gospel, with its liberating power, Christians were taught that the woman should be the helpmeet of the man, his equal under God. The Holy Spirit and his gifts were showered equally on the men and the women of the early church. Jesus himself had welcomed

women into his inner circle. They were last at his cross and
first at his grave. The first person he spoke to after his
resurrection was a woman.

Because of this, women responded to Christianity with cries
of joy; but as they rejoiced in their newfound freedom it
became apparent that the sacred ties of marriage were in
danger of being shaken. Especially in the case of those
women whose husbands were not Christians. F.B. Meyer
explains it this way: [16]

> This was the origin of the command to be in
> subjection. It was, primarily, addressed for those
> who since their marriage had become Christians.
> There was considerable hesitancy in the early
> church, as to their duty under such circumstances.
> 'Should they leave their husbands?' 'Should they
> alter their behaviour to them?' 'Should they assume
> any superiority?' 'No,' said the Apostles, 'stay where
> you are, however painful your position, and
> uncongenial your surroundings, and trying your
> husband's conduct. Be chaste, gentle, loving,
> submissive, winsome, so that hearts may be
> softened, which have never heard a word of Gospel
> preaching, and may be won by the beauty of your
> holy and unselfish lives.'

> Of course, where true love subsists between husband
> and wife, and where both are Christians, such a
> command as this is hardly needed. There is no room
> for subjection where there are no masterful
> commands, no standing up for rights; jealous strife
> for independence. The sensitive instincts of love
> define exactly, as no words could do the respective

---

[16] Meyer F. B; *Tried by Fire – Exposition of the First Epistle of Peter;* Oliphants,
Blundell House, London. 1970.

position of husband and wife...

And in the words of a more modern author:

> Submission is not the exclusive responsibility of the woman. Submission is the life-style of the Christian. To the woman the question is, are you willing to submit yourself, not first of all, to your husband, but to the Lord's plan for your functioning in the marital relationship? Don't let anybody fog you. If you cannot submit to your husband's leadership, then your problem is not only with your husband. Your problem is also with your Lord. You have not faced the basic issue of the Lordship of Christ. The filling of the Holy Spirit always involves submission to Christ. [17]

As Christian women with godly husbands who are willing to lay down their lives for us, as Christ did for the church, surely there need be no coercion to submit, *"as to the Lord"*.

I love Jill Briscoe's picture of a Christian home –

> I believe the Christian home should be like a womb, giving the growing embryo of our marriage a place to safely develop, a space to move and stretch, to cry and struggle until finally our relationship is fully developed and mature. [18]

Ministry

In her testimony in chapter five of this book, Joan Beard says –

"As the children grew, I was able to become more involved in the ministry."

Years ago, I had to speak to a group of pastors' wives, and I

---

[17] Hendricks, Howard and Jean; *Heaven Help the Home*. pg. 31.

[18] Briscoe, Jill; *Fight for the Family*; pg. 22.

presented diagrammatically what Joan is saying to us. Many young wives feel cut off from the ministry and yet are impatient to win the world. On the other hand, those whose children have grown up are able to agree with Joan. If only, as young mothers, we were not so bound by time and space, and could see things from God's perspective, we would not become so frustrated during the time our children are small.

Once again, I have found it helpful to present this diagrammatically. Starting from a single life when we can be available to God on a large scale if we choose, to the time when the children leave home, and once again we can do what we wish ideally. We should also take into consideration the great value to the kingdom of retired people. The curve in the following graph gives us hope, especially if we have a kingdom mentality. God is not in the same kind of hurry we are!

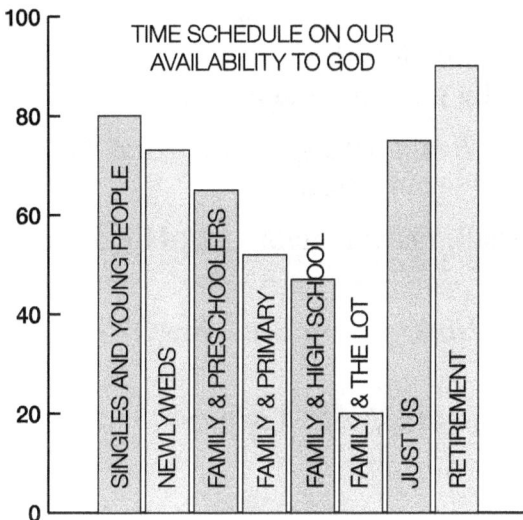

TIME SCHEDULE ON OUR AVAILABILITY TO GOD

Helpful Books

Arvella Schuller, *The Positive Family*; Berkley, 1982.

Howard and Jean Kendricks, *Heaven Help the Home*; Victor Books, 1960.

Barry and Vanessa Chant, *Straight Talk About Marriage*; Tabor, 1983.

Trobisch, *I Married You*; IVP, 1971.

Larry Crabb, *Men and Women*; Zondervan, 1991, also *The Marriage Builder*; Zondervan, 1983.

Devotional material for the whole family is available from places like Scripture Union. However, for families of very young children some helpful books are -

Gloria Gaither and Shirley Dobson, *Let's Make a Memory*; Word Books, 1983

William Coleman, *Singing Penguins and Puffed Up Toads; Counting Stars; My Magnificent Machine* (for pre-schoolers); *The Goodnight Book; Today I Feel Like A Warm Fuzzy*; (all these by William Coleman, Bethany, 1981-1984.

Stephen Barclift, *Beginner Devotional and Early Reader's Bible;* Questar Publisher, 1991.

Catherine Marshall, *Friends with God*; Hodder and Stoughton, 1981.

Effie Williams, *A Hive of Busy Bees;* Shaw Foundations Inc., 1969.

Allen Hart, *Jahsmann Little Visits with God*; Concordia, 1957.

Chapter Nine

The Pastor's Widow

When I decided to go ahead with the first edition of this book it was with the realization that there may be more to add at a later date. Sure enough, I have been confronted with another very important issue: The suffering of the pastor's widow and the difference between her lot and the experience of other widows. Real names have been avoided, but all the following stories are true experiences suffered by Pastors' widows.

The Dilemma of the Pastor's Widow

Fay and Robert were pastors of a large church in the USA. In their middle thirties they looked forward to many years of service for God. One morning Robert scheduled a business meeting from which he never returned. A massive heart attack cut short his life during the meeting. He was only 34 years of age! His wife and children were grief stricken; the congregation overwhelmed. The whole church mourned the suddenness of their pastor's death; his youth and promise cut off in such a tragic manner. They held a solemn funeral service and endeavoured to get on with their lives.

Since their church was an independent charismatic church, and Fay had a strong ministry of her own, the congregation decided to ask her if she would take over the church, which she did. After one year, however, she had to resign, as her children needed her undivided attention. She moved away from the area and another pastor was invited to take her place. Fay was thus bereft of her husband and her church, her friends of many years standing, and her support. She had to begin life anew in another state.

Mildred has a different story: She and her husband had a small church and she was part of the ministry team, but without any preaching skills. When her husband died, another pastor came to take over the church, and naturally she had to step aside. The new pastor's wife took over the duties that had been Mildred's and Mildred was left to get on with her life as best she could. Gradually the loyalty of the people was transferred to the new pastor and his wife. To suffer grief on the death of her husband was grief enough; to be cut off from her ministry was yet another loss, which Mildred felt keenly. It was a strange sensation, she felt somehow invisible, no one seemed to care whether she was there or not. It was not the fault of the people, merely the change in circumstances. No one knew quite what to do with Mildred. Eventually she moved to a different church and was welcomed there with open arms. Her ministry blossomed again, and she was made a visitation officer by her new pastor. He recognized her worth and she began to feel useful again.

Janet's story is a sad one: she and her husband had served the Lord together for many years and now they were retired and enjoying their last few years together. A new pastor had taken over their ministry, and they rejoiced in the fact that their former church was continuing in the blessing of God. After a short time of retirement, Janet's husband died, and Janet is now left alone. Although she lives close by her former church, the people she served for so many years of her life seem too busy to spend time with her. Her denomination has forgotten her. She looks back over the years of service and says to herself, *"Truly my reward is in heaven, I'm certainly not enjoying much of it here and now."*

Another sad story I heard recently concerned the widow of a Bible School principal. For many years she worked alongside her husband building the Bible School from nothing to a thriving enterprise. When her husband died, the faculty politely showed her the door. They removed her furniture from the building and left her to fend for herself. I suppose they said, *"Thanks for all your hard work."* However, this was no way to treat someone who had spent her life helping to build the School. After all those years of going without, of prayer, of faith, of counsel - she deserved something more than a polite, *"Goodbye."*

Of course, all stories are not this traumatic as some pastors' wives have large families to care for them and many are cared for by their congregation and not forgotten or cast aside. However, a significant number do feel there is a large hole left in their life when their pastor husband dies, and perhaps those of us who are not yet widowed, need to make ourselves more aware of those who are suffering loss.

Grief Comes to Us All

One thing is certain, that one day, according to statistics, there will be more widows than widowers left to continue their lives after having been in ministry. We should begin to take notice of what is happening to other pastors' widows. Can we hold out a helping hand, send a card, write a letter, visit and show some friendship.

Many people seem helpless in the face of grief. They say, *"I don't know what to say."*

It is so much easier to stay away than to visit and sit awkwardly, wondering what we should be saying or doing. Let me list some pointers that can help when anyone is suffering grief

At first when visiting, your presence is comfort enough. There is no need to speak; in fact, sometimes speaking can be the wrong thing to do. Especially if all you can think of are worn out phrases. Just to be there and give a comforting hug is enough.

As time goes on seek to be practical. If there are young children, offer to help with the housework, do some shopping, tidy the house; provide a meal. Later, as the widow regains her equilibrium and begins to take up these tasks for herself, an occasional phone call, or a card or letter would keep her feeling loved and cared for.

Some of us can be very supportive at the time of a death, but then later on we get busy, life goes on, and we tend to forget that the one left is still suffering; even more acutely, now that others have stopped coming and stopped offering help. After the initial deep sorrow, the years seem to stretch ahead, empty and lonely. This is the time when help would be most appreciated.

> It isn't for the moment you are struck that you need courage, strength is needed for the long uphill climb back to sanity, and faith, and security. [19]

> Grief has many faces, normal grief usually involves intense sorrow, pain, loneliness, anger, depression, physical symptoms, and changes in interpersonal relationships. However, not everyone suffers in the same way or in the same order of feeling. Some may suffer denial, fantasy, restlessness, disorganization, inefficiency, irritability. They may have a desire to talk considerably about the deceased and feel that life no longer has any meaning for them. However, if there are friends who understand, the time of grief is made bearable and the day comes when the Lord makes a way for life to continue. [20]

If the one suffering is a pastor's widow then she will need the same care and the same understanding as others, but there will be a difference. If she has been involved in ministry, she may wish to continue to do something for the Lord. Her home church should make some allowance for this, or if she desires to move to another church, perhaps in another city,

---

[19] Anne Morrow Lindbergh.

[20] Gary Collins; *Christian Counseling*, Word Publishing 1988.

then she should have all the support she needs to enter ministry of some kind if that is what she desires.

One pastor's widow remains in her home church and is very happy there; another moves to a new town and is used very successfully in visitation ministry; another assists her children, who are pastors, to build up a church; another becomes a missionary; another younger pastor's wife concentrates on bringing up her children. Everyone is different and lives in her own unique environment and has her own needs.

Let us be aware of the situation, using our compassion and practical abilities to aid the pastor's widow where necessary.

Divorce - When a Man Leaves the Ministry

Being a pastor's widow is sorrow enough; being divorced from a pastor is an even more tragic scenario. The divorcee also loses her ministry, her friends, her church, and sometimes she doesn't know why! What has she done, where has she gone wrong? Is she at fault? All these questions hammer at her mind. We need to try to understand how she feels, perhaps we can help a little.

I have a friend who suffered, not only the death of one of her children, but also divorce from her husband. She lost her son, her husband and her ministry in the space of two years. Her suffering was intense and there seemed to be no one to help her or minister to her. In fact, well-meaning friends only added to her grief. After intense suffering she was able to regain her equilibrium and through much agonizing prayer she rebuilt her life and brought her remaining children through to a vibrant Christian faith. She and her children are all serving God today in various ways.

The Lord is able and willing to give victory to those who trust in him and who lean on him in childlike faith. Though we can suffer with the Psalmist:

Save me, O God, for the waters are come up to my neck. I sink in miry depths, where there is no foothold. I have come into deep waters; the floods engulf me. I am worn out calling for help; my throat is parched. My eyes fail looking for my God (Ps 69:1-3).

We can finally rejoice with him,

Those who sow in tears will reap with songs of joy. He who goes out weeping, carrying seed to sow, will return with songs of joy, carrying sheaves with him (Ps 126:5-6)

Helpful Books

Kindah Greening, *Grief the Toothache of the Soul*, Healing Hurting Hearts Ministry, P.O. Box 477, Burleigh Heads, Queensland 4220, Australia. 1997.

Stan DeKoven, *Grief Relief*, Vision Publishing, Ramona CA.

Chapter Ten

On the Home and Family

The content of this chapter arises from material collected over 40 years of ministry, unfortunately some of it before I learned to keep a record of my sources. For this I apologise. I have tracked down some but not all the quotes, indeed there may be some sentences which are quotes and I ám unaware of this!

Character

Ancient Rome was built on the home and family. There was only one divorce recorded during the first 500 years. That divorce was caused by a man who wanted children, but his wife was barren, so he divorced her and remarried to have children.

Then Rome with her mighty army conquered Greece. Her soldiers were stationed there, and many Greek slaves were shifted to Rome to serve their new masters.

Gradually the Romans were corrupted by foreign influence and by ever increasing luxury. They descended into frenetic lust, and the home and family which, until that time, had been the backbone of the nation, began to disintegrate. Divorce became common. One woman was known to have had sixteen husbands. Young women began to refuse to marry, for they could see no reason to do so.

Today our lax society with its looser morals and the humanistic philosophies espoused by some universities and colleges, have twisted many lives. Houses, cars, riches and the "good" things of life have replaced truth, integrity, family, and home. Prominent politicians have been laughed at and derided for their honesty!

Today when the moral fibre of the nation seems to be disintegrating before our eyes, we need more than ever before to be aware that Jesus is Lord, and that he must be Lord of our lives.

Some Christians do not reach this stage therefore they have no joy. They have only enough Christianity to make them miserable, but not enough for overflowing peace and joy. They cannot enter into the declaration of the Psalmist:

> *You have made known to me the path of life; you will fill me with joy in your presence, with eternal pleasures at your right hand (Ps 16:11).*

What does it mean to say that Jesus is Lord?

Our modern perception of a king is quite unlike the real power a monarch possessed in ancient times. A king had the decision of life and death over his subjects. He demanded absolute loyalty and faithfulness, backed up by the life and riches of each subject. He demanded absolute obedience. What does this mean to us?

Are we completely loyal, faithful and obedient to our Lord?

You may have no gross sin in your life, but how do you react out in the marketplace; in your job, out there in the world? Are you willing to lose your job because of your integrity?

Our homes and families should be an example to others. We should be examples to our children. Let us take the test of love. We expect our children to be loyal, faithful, obedient, and full of integrity. God expects the same from us, for we are his children.

How do we measure up? There are five different kinds of sin mentioned in the Word of God.

Missing the target (Gr. "harmartia"). This means falling short of perfection. Have we been as good as we could have been? Have we reached our full potential in God?

Stepping across the line between right and wrong (Gr. "parabasis"). This means transgression. Do we always stay on the side of honesty? Do we never, by word or silence, twist, evade, or distort the truth? Do we always stay on the side of love, courtesy, unselfishness?

Slipping across (Gr. "paraptoma"). This means offence, more of a blunder than a deliberate act. Are we ever swept away by passionate sin? This form of sin is not as deliberate as stepping across.

Lawlessness (Gr. "anomia"). This means iniquity and occurs 70 times in the Psalms. It is the sin of one who knows what is right but deliberately chooses to do wrong.

A failure to pay what is due (Gr. "opheilema"). This means a failure in duty. [21]

It is good to make deliberate choices in life before we are challenged by a trial or temptation. Thus, we should decide that we will never commit adultery, never divorce, never tell a lie. Then when an opportunity for sin arises, we are ready to spurn it. We have already committed ourselves to truth, integrity, faithfulness, and loyalty. There should then be no conflict, no dwelling on, or dreaming about, possible actions to further the trial, and make it harder to resist.

A crisis does not make us, but it does reveal who we truly are deep down. Our character is not formed by the crisis times; rather it is formed by the choices we make day after day. Then again, although our actions may be right and good, we can be defeated repeatedly by our reactions to the daily grind, to life situations, and to other people's actions. Our

[21] William Barclay's Daily Study Bible, *Gospel of Matthew,* Vol. 1, pg. 221-223.

inner reactions, if they are ones of jealousy, resentment, hatred, fear, or self pity, can be hidden from others, but still bring defeat and ruin upon us.

If I plan and make sure my outward actions are all good and pleasant, that is good; but it is my spontaneous reactions, which are unplanned, that reveal my true character. As Jesus told his disciples,

> *What comes out of a man is what makes him 'unclean' (Mk 7:20).*

Our real problem is not external, but internal. The difficulties, the pressures, the adversities, and the disappointments we face cause reactions in us which, if revealed, show our true character, whether strong or weak.

Some people are controlled by others, they never initiate anything, only reacting to what others are saying or doing. Do not allow others to manipulate your actions; decide for yourself to live for God, and to forge your being after his principles.

How can we be a good example to others?

We must realise that each one of us has some influence on people around us. Every change in a person can be traced back to an individual who had influence. Think back over your own life to significant moments that changed you. A few words spoken can have a profound influence. You can make a significant contribution to the lives of others. Your life, your happiness can affect them. Statistics have shown that we each bring significant change to at least 162 people in our lifetime.

People need to see healthy happy Christians, with joyful and contented lifestyles and marriages.

There are four things we can teach others to help them maintain a happy marriage and family life -

Keep a positive outlook. A negative person drains and dejects others and makes it harder for them to succeed. Finally, to protect themselves, they begin to avoid that person. What a contrast happy, well adjusted persons make to family life. Everyone loves them and wants to be near them.

Assume God-given responsibilities. The principles of the Bible do work, but we must work them. We should decide that our marriage is going to work and go on from there. We need to make deliberate choices to follow the instructions given to us in the Word. If we do these things, where it is necessary for change to occur, the dynamics of our life will alter.

Concentrate on training your children during the first five years. You will reap great rewards if you spend time with them in the early years, when character is formed. There are many fine books available now to help in this task.

Practise God's presence in everything you do. The Jews have prayers for every occasion of life. They have prayers for morning and evening, prayers for going out and for coming in, prayers for when they see a mountain or a lake and so on. If you follow this practice you will be bringing God into every part of your daily family life (De.6:4-7). Christianity won't be a thing apart; your children will see it working.

Maturity remains the secret of a well-adjusted marriage. It delivers us from selfishness and from using our partner to satisfy us and our desires. It gives us the ability and willingness to act in a way that makes it easier to adapt to each other. It accepts full responsibility for its own actions and the consequences of its own decisions. It is able to persevere patiently and never give up. In the end we will have the kind of marriage we are willing to work and pray for, the kind we truly desire. Building a happy marriage is itself a ministry today. Learn the things that work for you, and then teach others what you have learned.

Your marriage is everyone's business! They need to see that marriage can work. It is the nation's business! Good families are the backbone of the nation. It is your child's business! If your marriage ends in divorce then it not only brings disintegration to you, but also can bring destruction to your child's personality.

Marriage is also God's business!

> *... You flood the Lord's altar with your tears. You weep and wail because he no longer pays attention to your offerings or accepts them with pleasure from your hands. You ask, "Why?" It is because the Lord is acting as the witness between you and the wife of your youth, because you have broken faith with*
> *her, though she is your partner, the wife of your marriage covenant. Has not the Lord made them one? In flesh and spirit they are his. And why one? Because he was seeking godly offspring. So guard yourself in your spirit, and do not break faith with the wife of your youth. 'I hate divorce', says the Lord God of Israel, 'and I hate a man's covering himself with violence as well as with his garment,' says the Lord Almighty. (Mal 2:13-16).*

Scripture shows that how we perceive God is tied up with our marriage, our family and our children -

If the father has no pity for his child, then Ps.103:13 will have no meaning for the child -

> *As a father has compassion on his children, so the Lord has compassion on those who fear him; for he knows how we are formed, he remembers that we are dust.*

If the mother does not comfort her child, then Is. 66:13 will have no meaning -

> *As a mother comforts her child, so will I comfort you.*

Pr.18:24 reveals God to be closer than a brother. Brothers are also part of the family. If there has been incest, then how will a sister feel about this text?

> *... There is a friend who sticks closer than a brother.*

Ep.5:25 reveals the true and godly husband, how could a woman resist loving and revering a husband who was willing to die for her as Christ died for the church?

> *Husbands love your wives, just as Christ loved the church and gave himself for her.*

God wants us to have happy families, and we can have them if Jesus is Lord of our lives and we allow him to form our character. Selfishness will go! We will love one another and be a marvellous example to all who so desperately need to be taught how to live.

Things to Do With Your Children

Take them for picnics; to the zoo, to the beach. Read stories to them. Seek to show that serving Jesus and loving him can be fun. Answer gladly any questions asked. Spend time with them; thus, building their self-esteem.

Realise being a witness doesn't mean running around neglecting home and family. It means living the Christian life as an example to others. Let them see Christianity works!

The Wife

During the days of the early church women gave of their time, their possessions, and their homes. Paul instructed Titus to bid the older women to be reverent, not to be gossips, to teach and train the younger women to love their husbands and children and to be sensible, chaste, domestic, kind and submissive to their husbands. And the reason? So the Word of God should not be discredited (Tit.2:3-5).

As a young wife for many years I thought God should be first in my life. I still feel this is correct; but then next on my list of priorities came the church. Being full of zeal for God I thought he and his church must be predominant in my life.

However, after much prayer and meditation and a few unhappy experiences I became convinced my list was wrong. God should come first, yes, but after that I should take care of my husband, myself and our children before making time for church related activities. This subject is much debated in our day and Vanessa Chant has covered this subject admirably in chapter eight of this book.

How did God show me what it means to be a good wife? First, he taught me to love myself, to work out a good self-image. Only then would I be set free to love my husband as he needed to be loved.

Together a man and a woman make up all the qualities of God; therefore, he taught me I needed to be a helpmeet to my husband (Ge.1:27; 2:18).

Usually a man has more logic and a woman more intuition so that, as husband and wife, they are able to work out their problems together. God gave us to our husbands for strength and support and the wise man will listen to his wife and weigh her words before making any important decision. We should complement each other and not compete against one another.

> He who finds a wife finds what is good and receives favour from the Lord (Pr.18:22).

Strive to live always so your husband will not regret choosing you as his helpmeet!

A wife is to be a companion to her husband. What a comfortable word that is. In those heart-breaking verses in Malachi 2:14, where God cries out against divorce, he calls the wife, "*your partner and the wife of your marriage covenant*". In Ecclesiastes 4:9 we read "*two are better than one*". If one falls the other will raise him, they keep each other warm and protect one another.

There are many very lonely people in this world. We are very blessed to have a husband, and more especially a Christian husband. Let us be a true companion, one in whom he can safely trust. If we sow love, we will reap love; if we sow kindness, we will reap kindness.

We must love our husbands as we are commanded to do in Tit 2:4. In the context of marriage in Bible days where marriages were arranged, love was something that followed marriage, it was something the wife chose to do or not to do. In our day we begin with love and sometimes it may be hard to continue to love, but we have no option. We must decide to love, and continue to love our husbands, no matter what vicissitudes we face. We have vowed to do so - "*For richer for poorer, in sickness and in health, as long as we both shall live.*"

I was horrified during our ten years in America to have some pastors confide in me that their wives controlled them by threatening to leave them and obtain a divorce. They faced the possible ruin of their ministry if they would not do everything their wife wanted.

We are taught in Ep. 5:33 to respect our husbands. This should be an easy thing for any wife whose husband is fulfilling the scriptural directions that refer to him, which show he is to love his wife enough to die for her, even as Christ died for the church (Ep 5:25).

Last of all a wife should learn from her husband. If a husband is fulfilling his duty to his wife, he will be setting her free to grow and develop and learn, just as he wants to grow and develop and learn. In doing this he will be loving her as he loves himself.

As women, we must be aware and deal quickly with hurts, bitterness, criticism, and jealousy, by taking them to the Lord and letting him heal us. If we don't do this, we can be miserable with self pity, which can then be a breeding ground for all kinds of unhappiness in our marriage. We cannot allow a day to go by without dealing with these things if it becomes necessary. We must keep short accounts with God and with our husband. If we do, we will have a happy and peaceful home that will be an example to all.

Finally, brothers, whatever is true, whatever is noble, whatever is right, whatever is pure, whatever is lovely, whatever is admirable - if anything is excellent or praiseworthy - think about such things (Ph 4:8).

The Mother

Her children arise and call her blessed; her husband also, and he praises her: Many women do noble things, but you surpass them all (Pr 31:28-29).

Listen, my son, to your father's instruction and do not forsake your mother's teaching. (Pr 1:8).

A family is a picture of the church and of Jesus' relationship with the church, so let him be your example. Provide a climate in your home in which love, trust, honesty and security can flourish. If you don't have this then all the material things you can provide will have no meaning. They will just bring frustration and anger to your children.

Trust and tenderness are fragile emotions; they cannot survive battering and bruising. People withdraw and retreat if they are hurt. Home must be a place where family members can give love without being hurt or taken advantage of.

Remember love is a doing word. You can't say you love someone and then do things that prove otherwise.

God chooses us to use us. There is no one else who can mother our children in the same way we can. If we leave this task undone it will not be done as well. Mothering our children is the next most important task for us women. Our first is to be loving and supportive toward our husbands. Our children are a gift to us from God, the greatest gift God can give to a man and his wife.

A child is one of life's greatest responsibilities, and each child contains treasure waiting to be revealed. We must give our children love first, then discipline. If we do this then our love will make up for our many blunders. None of us is perfect, and we must ask God to guide us every day.

Never be afraid to say those very important words, *"I'm sorry!"* or *"I was wrong!"* If you can admit your faults, then your child will gain the courage to admit his or her faults so they can be dealt with.

Let us look at Mary as an example of motherhood. She was a good example in three ways.

- **She was submissive to the will of God.**

  I am the Lord's servant," Mary answered. "May it be to me as you have said ... (Lu 1:38; see also Ps 40:8; 143:10).

Mary disdained the prayer of many people who want to change God instead of allowing God to change them. So we pray many times, *"May it not be your will,"* By contrast Mary was submissive and ready to agree with God. *"May it be to me as you have said,"* was her prayer. She was called to a most incredible task and she was ready. She was ready because:

- **She was full of the Word of God.**

I have hidden your word in my heart that I might not sin against you (Ps 119:11).

Mary was steeped in Scripture, learned at her mother's knee. She knew someone would be chosen to bear the Messiah. She knew she was descended from David and therefore there was a possibility she could be the chosen one. She was obviously familiar with Hannah's prayer in 1 Sam 2 for the Magnificat has echoes of Hannah's prayer.

The more we store the Word of God in our hearts the more we are renewed and freed from past guilty fears so that we can serve God. How important it is to teach our children right from the start of their lives the life-giving words of God, to fill their minds with good and pure thoughts. As we are taught in Colossians,

Let the word of Christ dwell in you richly, as you teach and admonish one another in all wisdom ... (Cl 3:16a).

- **She was overflowing with the joy of God.**

My soul glorifies the Lord and my spirit rejoices in God my Saviour (Lu 1:46-47).

Mary rejoiced in her God, and so can we. He has saved us from sin, from sickness, and from eternal death.

Rejoicing will keep us healthy and happy, and it will ensure a happy home life.

A cheerful look brings joy to the heart, and good news brings health to the bones (Pr 15:30).

Rejoicing will make it even more likely our children will learn to love God and follow him. They will learn their attitude toward God by watching us. Are you stern or loving, happy or sad? Remember you are their role model.

A child's basic needs for love and self worth are met by the mother from the day he or she is born. This is because she has the necessary equipment to nourish and nurture her baby.

> *Can a mother forget the baby at her breast and have no compassion on the child she has borne? (Is 49:15; see also Is 66:11-13; 1Th 2:7).*

In Bible days weaning took place between two and three years of age and it produced a very peaceful and contented child.

> *But I have stilled and quieted my soul; like a weaned child with its mother, like a weaned child is my soul within me (Ps 131:2).*

A mother teaches her children (Pr 1:8; 6:20). Her children bless her because she loves them (Pr 31:28; Tit 2:4).

The Husband

The Jews have a prayer which devout Jewish men still pray each morning.

"I thank you God that I was not made a Gentile, a slave or a woman".

In Bible days the status of women was very different from what it is today. Women were looked on as the property of the husband. Divorce was very easy and given for trivial reasons. Jesus came to change all of this; and Paul's remarks in Ep 5:22-23 raise the ideal of marriage to the highest level. Nowadays women have stepped down from this pedestal in their search for freedom. Many men no longer respect them as they used to do. Indeed, there is a great increase in the abuse of women.

In the book of Ephesians, Christian men are taught to love their wives sacrificially, even as Christ loved the church and gave his life for it. They are taught to cherish their wives and are forbidden to hate them.

A man's wife belongs to him. The Bible says she has been placed under him for her protection. He is not to coerce her or bully her but to protect and care for her. He is not to insist on his own way in everything but together they are to work out their problems with God's help. The wife in turn should be grateful for her husband's covering and protection and not rebellious under it.

On the other hand, a husband should be aware of the trust placed in him by God and measure up to it by his tender caring. The wife is not owned by her husband; only God can be said to own us, for he bought us with the precious blood of Jesus. However, she belongs to her husband, and in belonging to him she is in her rightful place.

I have lost the article now, but I remember reading one time of a non-Christian club in England, set up solely to teach good manners to couples. They claimed to have saved hundreds of marriages.

If husbands and wives would follow this simple rule of good manners, and reverse the usual trend, which is to be extra nice to the people outside of the family and atrociously rude to the partner to whom they should be loving and kind, then we would have some very beautiful, and restful, and supportive relationships within marriage.

Husbands and wives should pray for each other rather than criticise. Maybe your partner needs to change, but perhaps before God can change your partner, he needs to do something in you first. Other people change in relation to changes in us. Couples should accept one another as they are and not try to change each other. Only God can change an individual.

A lack of love and mutual submission can cause the Word of God to be discredited and our prayers to go unanswered.

Husbands, in the same way be considerate as you

live with your wives, and treat them with respect as the weaker partner and as heirs with you of the gracious gift of life, so that nothing will hinder your prayers (1 Pe 3:7).

Lars I. Granberg, president of North West College, Iowa, has these words to share:

Learning to give when we'd rather receive, forgive when we'd rather nurse a grudge, and love when we'd rather be loved, moves us toward Christian maturity.

This kind of Christian maturity leads to happiness in marriage.

The husband who is also a pastor needs to be especially careful of his wife. He needs to be protective. If he sees she is doing too much he needs to caution her, if he sees she is being attacked he needs to show his support for her. He needs to make it abundantly clear to all that she is first and foremost his support and encouragement and the mother of his children, before any extra demands are made of her.

He needs to make it plain that she and she only is the object of his love and regard, that he respects her and will not allow her to be hurt or taken advantage of.

If he will do these things, then she will be set free from the demands of others and able to set her own agenda. She will be far more relaxed, and happy to be a pastor's wife.

The Father

Listen my son, to your father's instruction and do not forsake your mother's teaching (Pr 1:8).

Fathers are very important to children; this truth is becoming more and more apparent as research continues. Many fathers have abandoned their role over the last twenty years, and we are now beginning to see just what a tragedy this can be. Fathers are vitally needed, by both sons and daughters. A weak or absent father can result in homosexuality in the sons and harlotry in the daughters.

What then does a Christian father need to do, and be, to protect his children from a disintegration of personality?

The most important thing is to love his wife, the mother of his children; to be there during her pregnancy, nurturing, protecting and providing for mother and baby. To speak to their baby while he or she is still in the womb, to pray for, and bless the baby even before he or she is born. In recent experiments it has been proved that babies can hear in the womb. Of course, they don't understand the words, but hearing the father's voice prepares them for hearing his voice once they are born. This helps with the bonding of father and child.

What is a father? In the Bible a father is described as one who encourages, exhorts, and comforts.

> *For you know that we dealt with each of you as a father deals with his children, encouraging, comforting, and urging you to live lives worthy of God, who calls you into his kingdom and glory (1Th 2:11-12).*

To urge means to use words or arguments to arouse or spur on to good deeds. To encourage is to give courage to, to give confidence to, to inspire. So, discipline is not all spankings and punishment but rather the positive task of exhorting and encouraging the children in our care.

Fathers also teach and train, bringing their children up in the discipline and the instruction of the Lord.

> *These commandments that I give you today are to be upon your hearts. Impress them on your children. Talk about them when you sit at home and when you walk along the road, when you lie down*

and when you get up (De 6:6-7).

Fathers, do not exasperate your children; instead, bring them up in the training and instruction of the Lord (Ep 6:4; see also Col 3:21).

A good father does not provoke his children until they get angry, but he disciplines his children with a firm kindness. Many times, the word discipline is used in the book of Proverbs. 75% of those verses refer to correction, rebuke, instruction or reproof, and only 25% indicate any form of physical punishment.

The foundation of discipline must be love. Discipline starts from the day a child is born because the foundation of discipline is love and trust. A baby whose cries are quickly responded to and whose needs are carefully met is a baby who feels loved and is developing trust.

How is this positive direction and self control developed in a child? It is created through unconditional love. It is easy to discipline a child who feels loved. The biggest task in discipline is to make the child feel the warmth of your love. Punishment is part of discipline but only a small part. Discipline is primarily training, instruction and correction.

Self esteem is built in this way:

(By) giving a child our full, undivided attention, in such a way that he feels without a doubt that he is completely loved. That he is valuable enough in his own right to warrant the parent's un-distracted watchfulness, appreciation and uncompromising regard. [22]

Currently teenagers and some adults have trouble with perceiving God as Father. This is because as a child their perception of God was shaped by their parents and so many

---

[22] Dr. Ross Campbell; *How To Really Love Your Child.*

have had abusive parents. If the parents' primary orientation toward their children is one of unconditional love, forgiveness and nurture, then the child will have a true perception of God. If, on the other hand, the parents' primary orientation is one of conditional love, judgment and punishment, the children will have a wrong understanding of who God is, and of his character.

Working as a pastor with children or fathering children, needs constant prayer, for their physical needs, emotional needs, and spiritual needs. It requires transparency. Struggles and mistakes need to be shared and sometimes forgiveness must be asked.

Behold children are a gift of the Lord (Ps 127:3).

> Successful family living strikes me as being in many ways like playing chamber music. Each member of the ensemble has his own skills ... but the grace and strength and sweetness of the performance come from everyone's willingness to subordinate individual skill and personal ambition to the requirement of balance and blend. [23]

Helpful Books

The Hurting Parent; Margie M. Lewis, (Zondervan).

How to Really Love Your Child & How to Really Love Your Teenager; Dr. Ross Campbell.

How to Live Almost Happily with a Teenager; Lois and Joel Davitz, (Collins; Dove).

Restoring the Christian Family; John & Paula Sandford, (Word Books).

---

[23] Annis Duffy.

Chapter Eleven

Unsung Heroines of History

Mary Livingstone

David Livingstone was a giant of the Christian faith, one of the first medical missionaries, a linguist, a geographer, an explorer, a crusader against slavery, and a naturalist, he had a robust and determined faith which showed itself in a thousand practical ways. But what of Mary his wife?

In answer to the question, *"What do you apprehend are the proper duties of a Christian missionary?"* David Livingstone wrote these words in relation to marriage-

> Unmarried: Under no engagement relating to marriage, never made proposals of marriage, nor conducted myself so to any woman as to cause her to suspect that I intended anything relating to marriage; and so far as my present wishes are concerned, I should prefer going out unmarried, that I might be without that care which the concerns of a family necessarily induce, and give myself wholly to the work. [24]

In the light of future events perhaps it would have been better for everyone concerned if Livingstone had kept to this decision. His wife Mary had much to endure because of his ministry.

While courting her he described her as, *"Not romantic but a matter-of-fact lady, a little, thick, black-haired girl, sturdy, and all that I want."* She also possessed refinement, delicacy,

---

[24]   George Seaver; David Livingstone His Life and Letters; Harper & Brothers 1957. pgs. 26, 86, 276, 412, 527.

and tact; qualities which he lacked.

Anyone who wished to keep up with the boundless energy of David Livingstone, and his desire to serve God by journeying into unknown parts of Africa, had to keep pace with him – or drop out. Mary tried to keep up, but it was impossible for any woman in that climate, and under those privations, to keep going. She didn't drop out, but she collapsed under the strain.

When Mary had given birth to their second child she and the children had to return to England and there wait for four long years for David. During this time Mary tried to care for their little ones in rented accommodation; she was broken in health, and sometimes she had no word from her husband for long stretches of time.

When Livingstone had been longest unheard of, her heart sank altogether; but through prayer, tranquillity of mind returned, even before the arrival of any letter announcing his safety.

Despite all these things Mary's love never wavered. This poem she wrote on her return to England encapsulates her devotion:

A hundred thousand welcomes, and it's time for you to come
From the land of the foreigner, to your country and your
home.
Oh, long as we were parted, ever since you went away,
I never passed an easy night, or knew an easy day.

Do you think I would reproach you with the sorrows that I
bore?
Since the sorrow is all over now I have you here once more,
And there's nothing but the gladness and the love within my
heart,
And the hope so sweet and certain that again we'll never
part.

A hundred thousand welcomes! How my heart is gushing o'er
With the love and joy and wonder thus to see your face once more.
How did I love without you these long years of woe?
It seems as if 'twould kill me to be parted from you now.

You'll never part me, darling, there's a promise in your eye;
I may tend to you while I'm living, you will watch me when I die;
And if death but kindly lead me to the blessed home on high,
What a hundred thousand welcomes will await you in the sky!

There followed years of separations, and although David wrote beautiful letters of consolation to Mary, these could not make up for the fact that, in twenty years of marriage, they had lived in a home together for only four of them. During the years of separation Mary suffered lapses of faith, and her letters to her husband tell of much spiritual darkness. They did have some brief times together and altogether they had four children. As soon as she was able to travel after the birth of her last daughter, in Kuruman, Mary returned to Scotland to be near her other children, Thomas, Robert and Agnes, who were attending school there. Mary loved her children and they loved her, but all the time she longed with a passionate intensity to be reunited with her husband.

Finally, after a few more years of loneliness, she insisted on joining him in Africa once again and they had a few weeks together before she finally caught a fever and died. David was shattered by her death and wrote in his journal-

> Oh, my Mary, my Mary! How often we have longed for a quiet home, since you and I were cast adrift at Kolobeng; surely the removal by a kind Father who

knows our frame means that he rewarded you by taking you to the best home, the eternal one in heaven...For the first time in my life I feel willing to die.

Towards the end of his life David wrote wistfully to his friend Oswell –

I hope you are playing with your children instead of being bothered by idiots. In looking back to Koloben I have one regret, and that is that I did not feel it my duty to play with my children as much as to teach the Bakwains. I worked very hard at that and was tired out at night. Now I have none to play with. So, my good friend, play while you may. They will soon be no longer bairns ...

It is a sad story, despite David's great achievements. His wife and children suffered by his absences.

Idelette Calvin

The great John Calvin had some very fixed ideas on marriage; not for him the beauty of face and figure that others craved.

This only is the beauty which allures me, if she is chaste, if not too fussy or fastidious, if economical, if patient, if there is hope that she will be interested about my health. [25]

After a few false starts, with his friends attempting to find him a wife, John finally found Idelette for himself. She was a widow with two children, a member of his own congregation and, besides having all the traits he desired, she was beautiful.

Calvin could not have found a better wife than Idelette, but

---

[25] Thea B. Van Helsema; *This Was John Calvin*, Baker Book House. 1981. pgs. 113, 147, 154, 155.

she, poor thing, scarcely ever had him to herself! She had to live in Calvin's student boarding house, and put up with his sharp-tongued house-keeper, but she didn't complain. Indeed, she was a very patient lady and eager to help her husband in any way. She visited the sick, comforted those in need, and shared her faith with others. Calvin was extremely happy in his wife.

Less than a month after the wedding both John and Idelette became ill and during the nine years of their otherwise happy union they were both frequently ill.

When Calvin was invited back to Geneva, Idelette set about making the house, which was provided by the church, into a home. They lived at Number 11 Canon Street and some furnishings were provided, others were arranged and added to by Idelette. In the back yard she established a vegetable garden and this, with the provisions given by the church, were enough to feed the family, consisting of Idelette, Idelette's daughter Judith, Antoine, Calvin's brother, and his wife and four children. Added to this large family group was the constant stream of visitors and messengers who stayed at Canon Street from time to time.

In the midst of these constant interruptions Calvin continued to write, preparing sermons and lectures and completing his important writings.

In 1542 plague struck Geneva and terror prevailed. Calvin offered to go to the great hospital and pray for the dying, but the church refused to allow it as they had great need of his services; besides Idelette was expecting their first child. Sadly, their little son Jacques was born prematurely and only lived for two days. Idelette did not recover fully from this blow.

A remark by Calvin shows us the attitude of pious Christians at this time when sickness and premature death were so frequent –

> The Lord has certainly inflicted a severe and bitter
> wound in the death of our infant son. But he is
> himself a Father and knows what is good for his
> children.

Altogether they had three children, but they all died at, or soon after, birth. Slowly Idelette's health deteriorated, but despite this it was she who brought peace and blessing into the home. When she was fit she would receive visitors, and even when she was not well no-one was turned away. Her hospitality was well known to all.

Even though he was seldom well Calvin was an intensely busy man, up at five each morning and busy all through the day, even when confined to bed he would continue working with books spread all over the quilt. Idelette was just the kind of wife he needed, quiet and peaceful and full of comfort.

In March of 1549 Idelette became deathly ill and lay peacefully waiting to die. She was not one to complain. Some of her last words were, *"O glorious resurrection. O God of Abraham, and all of our fathers, in thee have the faithful trusted during so many past ages, and none of them have trusted in vain. I too will hope."*

Calvin's words to a trusted friend on the death of his wife were these, *"Truly mine is no ordinary grief, I have been bereaved of the best companion of my life."*

Katherine Luther

Luther was 41 years of age when he married. He was a leading defender of the dignity of women and the goodness of marriage, but for a long time he resisted marrying as he was expecting to be martyred as a heretic. Then suddenly he decided to marry Katherine Von Bora, whom he had known for one year. She was one of a group of nuns who had escaped the cloister.

Katherine immediately began to make Luther comfortable. Before his marriage his bed had not been made for a whole year and was quite filthy. He himself suffered quite extensively with various illnesses, such as gout, insomnia, catarrh, hemorrhoids constipation, stones, dizziness, and ringing in the ears. Kate, to counteract this, became adept at using herbal remedies, poultices and massage.

Because Luther had no idea how to manage money and was always giving away all his things, Katherine had to take things into her own hands, even going so far as to hide articles from him so that he could not give them away. Their home was always overflowing with people; students, boys, girls, and older women, who needed a home and protection. Katherine presided over this large group with tact and great patience.

In her spare times she planted their fields, cared for an orchard, harvested a fish pond, and attended to the other multitudinous tasks of a farm.

They had six children including Elizabeth who died as a baby. They were Johannes (1526), Magdalene (1529), Martine (1531), Paul (1533) and Margaretha (1534). So many children and so quickly! Luther had to help out by washing the diapers and was not in the least ashamed to do it.

To their great sadness two of their children died, Elizabeth at eight months and Magdalene at the age of thirteen.

Katie, as she was affectionately called, was a redoubtable lady. Once when Luther shut himself away to study for three days, she took the door of his office off the hinges! Luther was heard to say, "*In domestic affairs I defer to Katie. Otherwise I am led by the Holy Ghost.*" He called his wife "*the morning star of Wittenberg*" as her day began at 4.00 am. She earned his respect because she excelled in business, she was a model housewife and a good business woman who kept their ministry to the poor and neglected from overwhelming their finances.

Luther's accolade to Katie is found in his last will and testament in which he, contrary to the common Germanic practice of appointing a male trustee to administer an estate, left her heir to everything!

Dorothy Carey

William Carey married Dorothy Plackett when he was only nineteen and she was twenty-five. Dorothy could not read or write and marked her marriage certificate with an X. Two years later their first little one, Ann, died and William himself was gravely ill, though he recovered. Over the next several years three more boys were born, Felix, William Jnr. and Peter, then another little girl, Lucy, who soon died, then Dorothy became pregnant again! It was hard in those days to prevent pregnancy and many had far larger families.

Poor Dorothy, when William Carey decided to go to the mission field of India, she already had three children with a fourth on the way! We must sympathise with her doubts that God was calling her to make such an enormous sacrifice; to go to that strange land, where there were so many unknown dangers for her family.

In the eighteenth century a wife and children were looked upon as the property of the husband. Therefore, it was the decision of William Carey alone to leave everything and go to India for life! Not that they were leaving much; they lived in abject poverty in England before their departure. William was a shoe-maker and unable to earn enough to keep his family in comfort. He was also pastor of a tiny Baptist church and this took up quite a lot of his time. There is no evidence that Dorothy resented this, but the thought of going to India was too much. She refused to be a part of the venture!

William wanted to leave immediately, never to return. Dorothy could not bear the thought of leaving family and the friends of a lifetime to go so far away, especially as monetary support was woefully lacking. Even if they survived the journey, would they succumb to the diseases of the tropics? Would their children be spared? She and William had already suffered the deaths of two daughters, so she knew the agony of losing a child.

William insisted on leaving anyway and resolved on taking their oldest son, Felix, with him. He abandoned his pregnant wife and the other two little children and boarded the vessel *Oxford* to begin his voyage to India. His companion, John Thomas, with his wife and daughter, had to delay the voyage while they paid some debts, and this time was used to persuade Mrs Carey to come after all. By this time poor Dorothy had given birth to another little son, Jabez, and allowed herself to be talked into going if her sister would come with her. The group finally took ship on a Dutch vessel. Dorothy was to bitterly regret her decision.

In the years that followed she grew more and more resentful of their life in India. Poverty, illness and loneliness each took their toll and when the sister finally married and moved away, and then shortly afterwards five year old Peter died of dysentery, Dorothy grew mad with grief. Her mental condition became worse and when in 1796 she gave birth to another son, Jonathon, she was described, by another missionary, as insane.

Dorothy suffered from delusions that her husband was having affairs with other women, sometimes she would follow her husband into the street, yelling at him, and at other times she would attack him physically. She was insanely jealous.

As time passed, she had to be confined. Amazingly, William Carey continued to translate the scriptures while she ranted and raved in the next room. Observing that Carey was an ineffectual father, a colleague, Hannah Marshman, sought to provide a motherly influence, and William Ward, another colleague, served as a surrogate father. This left Carey to continue his great work.

On Tuesday December 8th, 1807, Dorothy passed away peacefully without regaining her reason.

Although William Carey was known as the 'Father of Modern Missions' and his work was vital in that he and his associates translated the Bible into 48 languages and dialects of India and the East, it must be conceded that he was a failure in his family life. [26]

To be fair to Carey, he was like a lot of great men who are driven by a vision to do incredible things for God, hopelessly impractical! If he had waited until there was enough money to provide adequately for his family, if he had chosen a partner who was more business-like, he could have saved himself and his family from much unnecessary suffering, and perhaps Dorothy's reason would not have given way as it did. We do not know, and we cannot judge from this distance.

Carey did marry twice more before he finally passed away himself, and those two marriages were very happy and successful.

---

[26] Tucker, Dr. Ruth A.; art. William Carey's Less-Than-Perfect Family Life, Christian History, Issue 36, Vol Xl, No. 4.

Addendum One

These last pages are the results of the research paper I have asked pastors' wives and women leaders in churches in Australia and New Zealand to fill out over the past two years. This first list is from women in leadership:

Special Concerns of Women in Christian Leadership

1. They are concerned about the lack of training and opportunities to get together with other leaders for encouragement, help, further training, and inspiration.

2. Some have received training but still feel the need for refresher courses and the opportunity to share together and learn from one another. Those younger than 40 years of age had received far more training than the older ladies and this is a good sign and gives hope for the future.

3. Their helpful advice for other leaders:

- Take each day as it comes, never give up.
- Read books on leadership.
- Listen to others and learn from them.
- You have been called, so God will provide the ability.
- Don't lose your sense of humour.
- Be punctual.
- Be loyal to your leaders, try to see and understand the vision and direction of the pastors and leaders of the church.
- Don't take things too personally when someone is angry.
- Don't carry other peoples' hurts and problems; learn to give them over to the Lord.
- Remember to spend time alone with God. Don't get too busy so that you neglect prayer. Rely on the Holy Spirit for direction.

- Seek advice from some other women in leadership before you begin.
- Find someone to relate to and share with.
- Seek personal ministry when necessary.
- Accept the fact that you may fail sometimes and learn from your failures.
- Continue learning, reading, studying so you have something to give.
- Request advice and training for the specific task you are asked to do. Advice tailored to your needs and experience.
- Your first duty, if you are married, is to your husband and children, don't neglect them.
- Support your husband.
- Don't be afraid.
- Be a God-pleaser, not a man-pleaser.
- Learn to delegate.

4. The areas most difficult to handle

- People who like to be the centre of attention.
- Having to transport people to meetings and so being rushed and flurried when arriving.
- Seeing people I had grown close to leaving the church.
- Pressures of time.
- My husband complaining that church takes too much of my time.
- Maintaining motivation.
- Standing against discouragement.
- No access to any kind of leadership meetings.
- People rejecting you because of your leadership.
- Challenges from God.
- People who think they know it all and aren't open to teaching.
- The desire to hide and not go into leadership, to back

off.
- Overcoming a sense of inadequacy.
- Getting people to overcome their shyness and worship God aloud and with enthusiasm.
- Song leading, leading worship, counseling.
- Getting the study discussion back on track after it got off the track.
- Some pastors' and leaders' misunderstandings and treatment of us.

5. The best part of being a leader

- It gives me more confidence.
- It helps me to understand people.
- Seeing women change, being able to give out to others.
- To care for people, to make disciples, to see them mature and become strong in God.
- Being where God wants me.
- Fulfilling the will of God.
- The opportunity to use and develop spiritual gifts.
- Being able to express compassion/empathy as a woman to other women.
- Helping shy people to be more outgoing.

6. The worst part of being a leader

- Dealing with rowdy children during meetings.
- Being separated from my husband for leaders' retreats.
- Having no older woman to help me and relate to me.
- Trying to find a quiet room in which to counsel people.
- Having people judge you constantly.
- Having to give when you don't feel like it.
- Being used by people.
- Getting too busy for your family.

- Feeling I need to be available to everyone.
- Pulling people up without hurting their feelings.
- Being deserted by leaders when at a point of crisis.

7. Special Comments:

- Leaders should have their own house in order first and make sure they are giving adequate time to husband and children before they attempt to teach others.
- Being a leader is a privilege and a great responsebility, not to be taken lightly.
- Be careful not to give wrong advice to people. Let them make their own decisions after counseling.
- Remain teachable.

8. Being a leader is often challenging and stressful and many times unrewarding, yet serving God is one of the greatest honours I could ever hope for.

9. Working in the area of counseling, I find it difficult to keep motivated and stand against discouragement.

10. Make sure that as leaders we always present the things of God with love and zeal, not allowing ourselves to become lazy or weary but serving the Lord joyfully.

Results of Research on Pastors' Wives

These results came from a series of questions put to pastors' wives during the last three years.

1. Training:

Fifty-five percent of the pastors' wives who filled out my questionnaire had received some Bible school training; the rest had received no training at all. Only five felt they had received any specific training as a pastor's wife. Another three were pastors' daughters, so altogether eight had some preparation! No wonder there are burned out, disillusioned, bitter women who have taken their husbands out of ministry!

2. Advice received:

Sixty-one percent received no advice from anyone. Of the other 39%, 6 received help from other pastors' wives and the rest received help from Leaders' conferences. Imagine! 61% received no help from anyone. Only 39% received any help at all! Those who have received helpful advice have been sincerely grateful. It has made a tremendous difference to their lives.

In the questionnaire I asked them what helpful advice they would give other pastors' wives.

The single most repeated piece of advice was, *"Be yourself! Be a God-pleaser, not a man-pleaser. Live your life to please God not as people would like you to live. Don't let people place you in a mould!"*

Other advice they offered included the following; note how the variety of advice given shows how different we are from one another. Advice is affected by age, position, and by the size of the church:

3. Helpful advice they would like to give others:

- Be a good wife and mother first. Support your husband.
- Be yourself, find your ministry gift and pursue that and enjoy it. Don't try to please people, please God.
- Be a good listener.
- Know when to say no and when to delegate. Balance those comfortably.
- Ask lots of questions and learn from older pastors' wives.
- Communicate with your husband on all levels and on all subjects.
- Try not to take the problems of the church on yourself, give them to God, otherwise it can affect your family.

- Keep a guard on your personal relationships
- Don't give up.
- Don't try to copy anyone else.
- Live by the Word.
- Let the Lord mould and change you where necessary.
- Encourage your husband in his ministry.
- Seek God and extend yourself.
- Stay close to your husband and develop your relationship. Pray together.
- Remember, husband and children are top priority.
- Learn when to say "no". Know how to delegate.
- Don't be pressured to do something. Know God has called you. Don't feel guilty because you can't do something.
- Give God the problems, don't try to carry them yourself.
- Don't try to fulfil others' unreal expectations.
- Don't be a jack-of-all-trades, and don't cut yourself off from the church.
- Don't be dominated by the opinions of others but do listen.
- Believe that in his plan God intended you to be a pastor's wife.

4. Areas most difficult to handle?

- Pressure of people's expectations on what I should be doing.
- Criticism, people leaving the church.
- Taking a meeting
- My husband away at important times in the life of the children.
- The feeling that I am supposed to be available for anything and everything.
- Being seen as part of the "ministry team" and not as an individual, so not appreciated.

- Confronting people.
- Criticism of my husband.
- Listening to hurting and dissatisfied people and encouraging them to go back to Jesus rather than from person to person.
- Self expectations
- Balancing home life with spiritual and church life.
- Our home becoming like a "railway station", causing lack of time with the children, and lack of time for prayer and Bible study.

5. The best part of being a pastor's wife?

- The achievement of ministering and seeing people grow in God.
- Being a friend, support, and encouragement to my husband.
- Being able to speak into people's lives, to be an example and encouragement to them.
- The happiness I share with the women in the church.
- Working together with my husband to fulfil God's plan for our lives.
- Having a responsible role in seeing the church grow.
- Watching my husband develop in ministry and seeing my children grow up to serve the Lord.
- Seeing people grow in God and being able to help others.
- Being the wife of a godly man who understands his role as a husband.

6. The worst part of being a pastor's wife?

- Lack of advice and direction
- The feeling of being bound, that there is no escaping other's expectations.
- Handling leadership pressures, correction, gossip etc.
- Pressure of people's needs; pressure of time, balanc-

ing the needs of family with the needs of others.
- Criticism of my husband
- Being overworked
- Seeing people leave the church.
- People not liking something said or done by my husband. Gossip and slander.
- Feeling scrutinised, always being on show, the expectations of people on my children.
- Expectations of people, all different, sometimes I feel fragmented.
- Being separated from the family because of ministry travel.

7. What do you see as your main role?

- Working with my husband to benefit the church.
- Being a support and encouragement to my husband.
- Being a good wife and mother.
- To be an encourager in a one-to-one ministry.
- To provide a safe place for my husband.
- Youth, music and hospitality.
- Working with children and older women.
- A mother figure.
- Being an example in character, as a home maker, and in looking after my children.
- Teaching the women to be all they can be by grasping God's principles.
- To be a support for my husband, teaching other pastors' wives.
- Counseling, pastoral visitation, hospitality.

It is interesting to note the similarities and also the subtle differences in the answers given by the women in leadership and the pastors' wives. I think it is quite clear that there is a difference between being a leader of women and being a pastor's wife. The leader is there because this is her decision; she has more confidence and has chosen to serve. The pastor's wife on the other hand is thrust into her position whether she will or no, and as we have observed too many times without adequate preparation. I hope that this little book will go a long way toward helping pastors' wives to cope with their position.

Addendum Two

This research was compiled by Pastor Rob and Liz Bailey from their ongoing involvement with their "Camps for Pastors' Kids." Rob and Liz have been holding these camps for seven years and have directly influenced 150 young people whose parents are in ministry. The following statements come from the Pastors' Kids who enjoyed the camps run by Rob and Liz.

The Advantages of Being a P.K.

1. Spiritual rewards

- There are opportunities to closely relate to godly visiting ministries.
- There is access to a live-in pastor for prayer and counseling.
- There is an inherited anointing.
- We have a Christian heritage from godly parents who provide godly foundations
- We have parents who are making an effort to be good marriage partners and successful parents.
- We have protected lifestyles.
- We get encouragement and finance to learn musical instruments
- We have opportunity to be a witness to changes in people's lives.
- We share special moments in people's lives.
- We learn sensitivity to others.
- We have opportunities to learn faith through many testings.
- We are always being prayed for by visiting speakers and people in the church.
- We have opportunities to learn Scriptures well.

2. Material things

- We are eligible for Austudy because our parents are on a low income
- We receive birthday and Christmas presents from 'grannies' in the church.
- We are given gifts because people want to get sweet with the pastor.
- We are given food and 'hand me downs.'
- Our parents have good clothes we can borrow
- We get good seats at church concerts.
- We get to use church equipment.
- We are allowed a price reduction at private schools.
- The church pays certain bills.
- We have access to pastor's mail, magazines etc. from all the mailing lists.

3. Personal benefits

- Prestige.
- We are treated with respect (sometimes).
- People accept our leadership, and this forces us to develop.
- We get responsibilities earlier.
- We are trusted more than other kids the same age as we are.
- We get opportunities to minister without the 'proving' time that new people must go through.
- People trust us and tell us personal things.
- People accept our opinion.
- We act as a link between the Youth groups and older people.
- We often have the house to ourselves.

The Disadvantages of Being a P.K.

1. Expectations -

- We are expected to be perfect by imperfect people.
- We are expected to be present at everything.
- We are expected to work the hardest and to take the most responsibility.
- We are expected to know the Bible really well.
- We are expected to be an example to the other kids.
- We are expected to be part of a model family.

Lack of identity –

You are known for who your parents are and not for who you are yourself.

Your parents –

Can't separate themselves from being the pastor or the pastor's wife in their treatment of you.

4. Constant interruptions -

5. Peer group problems –

Your peers don't love you for yourself or see you as an individual. Hence – teasing, belittling, jealousy, and isolation, you are seen as a 'goody goody.'

6. You see your parents –

Hurt, criticized, manipulated, rejected, disappointed, and disillusioned.

7. People resent or hate you because they resent or hate your parents.

From Pk's to Those Starting in Ministry

*The following is a written record taken from a discussion that took place among 55 pastors' children aged between 14 and 25 years on how they feel PK's would like to be treated.

- Don't suffocate them – give them appropriate freedom
- Don't neglect them.
- Be supportive
- Have the attitude that the children's needs count – they are part of your ministry.
- Don't talk about church matters at the dinner table (or in front of the children at all).
- Try to keep the children separate from 'the ministry.'
- Have a night with the family each week (not just for spiritual input).
- Don't use your children as an example during your sermons (unless they give you permission).
- Don't load them up with everyone else's problems.
- Show an interest in what your children do.
- Don't expect too much from them e.g. don't expect them to be at every meeting and don't ask twenty questions if they don't attend!
- Watch that your house doesn't turn into a hotel.
- If possible, counsel away from the home e.g. church office. PK's feel that using the home for counseling is an invasion of their private space.
- Don't invite people for breakfast.
- Be sensitive to your children when others are around e.g. discipline them in private, don't draw attention to them from the pulpit.
- Don't make your children do all the work.
- Don't hold them up as an example to others.
- Don't force them into leadership.
- Check hypocrisy in yourself, e.g. being a different person at church than at home.
- Don't say to your kids, "*If you stuff up, it will make us look bad,*" or "*It won't look right to others*" or, "*What about our image,*" or "*You shouldn't do that – you're a PK*". The only criteria for behaviour is,

"What would Jesus do."

- Don't expect your kids to adhere to a dress code, e.g. girls in dresses only, guys in suits.
- Don't ask us to stand up and sing the latest songs as a family – we object!
- Don't be offended, intimidated or jealous if your children want to confide in or get advice from another adult, e.g. the Youth Pastor, rather than yourself.
- Don't force your kids to talk; don't pry.
- Be like a father and not a pastor when talking to your children.
- Don't Bible bash your children's friends e.g. giving them Scriptures, tapes, or talks.
- Get someone else to pray for your children at the altar, unless they particularly want you to pray.

Conclusion

You can't know what it is like to be a pastor's child! Your child is not treated in the same way as everyone else at all times!

Helpful Books

Robert M. Hicks, *The Christian Family in Changing Times,* Baker Books, 2002.

Beverley Lahaye, *How to Develop Your Child's Temperament,* Harvest House Publishers, 1977.

Dorothy Corkille Briggs, *Your Child's Self Esteem,* Doubleday 1970.

Diana Langberg, *Counsel for Pastor's Wives,* Ministry Resources Library, 1988.

www.ingramcontent.com/pod-product-compliance
Lightning Source LLC
Chambersburg PA
CBHW052003090426
42741CB00008B/1534